THE SNOWFLAKE GENERATION

How Fragility is the New Norm

PATRICK BASS

The Snowflake Generation: How Fragility is the New Norm
Copyright © 2024 by Patrick Bass

Dedication

To all the snowflakes, Kens, and Karens of Gen Z and beyond: You are the living, breathing cautionary tales of a society that traded grit for grievance, strength for sensitivity, and resilience for entitlement. May your fragility serve as a stark reminder of what happens when comfort is valued over character, and self-righteousness trumps responsibility. You are the true examples of what not to become, and it is your legacy that this book seeks to dismantle.

Table of Contents

FOREWORD

To truly understand the issue at hand, we must first define what we mean when we say "snowflake." The term refers to a derogatory label representing a cultural trend of fragility. A snowflake in Generation Z represents an individual who believes themselves to be entirely unique and precious, so much so that any hardship, challenge, or discomfort becomes intolerable. It's not simply a critique of individuality; individuality has always been an essential part of the human spirit and progress. It condemns the mindset that equates uniqueness with exemption from adversity and demands the world to adapt to the smallest inconveniences or discomforts.

Gen Z, often dubbed the "Snowflake Generation," has shown itself to be, in many respects, a product of an indulgent upbringing and a society too afraid to say "no." Wrapped in bubble wrap from the moment they could walk, they are protected not just from physical harm but also from the emotional complexities of failure, struggle, and personal accountability. The well-intentioned efforts to boost self-esteem and create a comfortable environment have inadvertently created individuals whose coping mechanisms are fragile at best, leaving them ill-equipped to handle the real world.

Snowflakes melt under pressure. And what we're witnessing now is an entire generation struggling to withstand the heat of adversity. When challenges arise, whether in work, relationships, or personal growth, the instinct is to crumble, to retreat, or to demand that others soften the blows of reality. Shielded from criticism by a culture that equates disagreement with personal attack, this generation's collective fragility has fostered a dangerous aversion to discomfort. But life is discomfort; it is through discomfort that we grow, adapt, and become better versions of ourselves. Gen Z's inability to tolerate this is leading us toward a troubling societal stagnation, one that threatens not only individual potential but the collective future of our nation.

This snowflake mentality has not stayed confined to Gen Z alone. It has infiltrated the broader societal landscape, seeping into the psyches of older generations who now also clamor for the same coddling and accommodations. This phenomenon has given rise to the well-known "Karen" and "Ken" archetypes adults who, much like their younger counterparts, are entitled, demanding, and quick to perceive themselves as victims when faced with even the most mundane of inconveniences. It is important to note that these behaviors did not happen by chance; they were purposefully executed.

The core of this book is not just to criticize for criticism's sake. This is not just a rant about what is wrong with young people today. It is a deeper exploration of what led us here, how the best intentions have paved a road toward fragility and entitlement, and how we might recalibrate. It's a call to abandon the comfort of victimhood in favor of resilience; An invitation for Gen Z to embrace resilience and make a meaningful impact.

Through this book, we will explore how this snowflake phenomenon developed, how it affects not just individuals but entire communities, and most importantly, how we can change course. We will confront uncomfortable truths, but only by doing so can we reverse the decay that entitlement and fragility have wrought upon our society. This is a rallying cry for those who reject snowflake culture and believe in embracing challenges for true growth.

The objective extends beyond mere survival; By understanding and addressing the "snowflake" mentality head-on, we can rebuild a generation and a nation that is strong, resilient, and purposeful. Achieving this brings us closer to reclaiming our formidable values: perseverance, discipline, and a shared purpose.

This is our opportunity to rewrite the narrative to transform the Snowflake Generation into the Phoenix Generation, rising from the ashes of fragility with newfound strength and purpose. The journey will not be easy, and it will not be comfortable. But it is necessary, and it is possible. And it starts here.

Introduction

A Warning from History

History is filled with the ruins of once great civilizations, each of which crumbled under the weight of its own success. From the Roman to the Ottoman Empire, societies that rose through struggle and innovation ultimately fell victim to the very comforts and luxuries their achievements afforded them. As these civilizations became more prosperous, they grew complacent. Over time, their citizens became dependent on government, on luxury, and on the assumption that their security was permanent. This cycle of rise and fall, meticulously outlined by Sir John Glubb in his essay The Fate of Empires, serves as a dire warning to all nations: no matter how powerful, every great civilization follows this trajectory. From the struggles of pioneers and the victories of military conquest to the flourishing of intellectualism and wealth, each society eventually crosses into decadence, where decay begins.

America now stands at a similar critical juncture. The warning signs are everywhere: the obsession with personal comfort, the widespread sense of entitlement, and an increasing reliance on government support. These symptoms of decline are not mere echoes of distant historical lessons; they are active, modern realities shaping the future of the United States. Contemporary American culture unmistakably mirrors the patterns that led to the fall of past empires. Without significant change, the future looks increasingly precarious.

SIR JOHN GLUBB'S FRAMEWORK: THE FATE OF EMPIRES

In his essay, Glubb outlined six distinct stages through which empires pass. These stages form a cycle that can be seen across different civilizations, from the early empires of Mesopotamia to modern European powers. Each empire, regardless of its historical context, follows a predictable path from pioneering ambition to ultimate decay.

- **Age of Pioneer**s: Empires are born through courage, exploration, and often through acts of conquest, as societies strive to expand and secure new territories.

- **Age of Conquests**: Military strength and strategic vision drive further expansion, solidifying the empire's dominance.

- **Age of Commerce**: Once expansion slows, focus shifts to trade, economic growth, and prosperity.

- **Age of Affluence**: Economic success leads to cultural and technological advancements, but also fosters luxury and indulgence.

- **Age of Intellect**: Intellectual pursuits challenge traditional values, promoting individualism and liberal ideals over collective responsibility.

- **Age of Decadence**: Complacency and excess set in. Civic duty erodes, personal indulgence becomes a cultural norm, and society becomes increasingly dependent on government support.

In the final stage, decadence, the vitality that once fueled a civilization's growth fades. Reliance on government assistance grows, personal comfort is prioritized over civic responsibility, and national pride gives way to selfishness and entitlement. The empire, having lost its way, collapses from within.

Today, America fits uncomfortably within this framework. The traits that once built the nation self-reliance, sacrifice, and discipline are being replaced by entitlement, a culture of instant gratification, and a dangerous dependency on government support. Unless drastic action is taken to reverse this trend, America may well follow the same path as the Romans, the British, and the Ottomans.

MODERN DAY AMERICA: A SOCIETY ON THE BRINK

America's history is one of pioneering ambition and relentless expansion. From the nation's founding, Americans pursued freedom and prosperity with unmatched fervor, achieving dominance as a global economic and military superpower. But in recent decades, signs of internal decay have become increasingly clear. The Age of Affluence, which propelled America to the forefront of world power, has given way to a modern consumer culture that places individual comfort above collective strength. The markers of decline are clear.

One of the most troubling indicators is the rise of entitlement and dependency. Data from the Pew Research Center shows a dramatic increase in reliance on government programs, particularly in the aftermath of the 2008 financial crisis and the COVID19 pandemic. What was once seen as a temporary safety net has, for many, become a way of life. Americans, like citizens in past empires, consider government support a lasting entitlement rather than a means to encourage self-sufficiency.

Cultural decay is another prominent sign. The breakdown of civil discourse, epitomized by the rise of "cancel culture," and the growing obsession with comfort and consumption, reflects a society that values personal gratification over collective responsibility. This cultural shift is eerily reminiscent of the Roman Empire's reliance on "bread and circuses" to distract the population while its internal structures weakened. In modern America, the parallels are striking. A culture consumed by entertainment and material wealth has supplanted the once strong ethos of civic duty and national pride.

Finally, the weakening of civic responsibility presents a dire threat to America's future. Each successive generation appears less connected to the idea of national duty. Public discourse is polarized, and younger generations increasingly turn to government intervention as the solution to societal problems, eschewing personal responsibility in favor of external reliance. This shift reflects a broader cultural decline in which resilience, accountability, and self-reliance are no longer prioritized. Instead, comfort and convenience have become the defining values.

HISTORICAL EXAMPLES OF CIVILIZATIONAL DECLINE

The path that America now treads is not new. History is replete with examples of once mighty empires that fell into the trap of decadence and ultimately crumbled.

The Roman Empire, at its height, was the most powerful society in the world. Yet, as it became more affluent, its citizens grew increasingly dependent on government handouts and entertainment to sustain them. "Bread and circuses" pacified a population that no longer felt the need to contribute to the state's wellbeing. Gradually deteriorating, the empire's military strength, economic power, and social fabric led to the collapse of Rome under the weight of its own excess. There are parallels to modern America. The nation's growing reliance on social welfare programs and its obsession with consumption over contribution mirror the very factors that led to Rome's decline.

Similarly, the British Empire, once the largest empire in history, decayed from within, long before its external collapse. Economic overextension, political polarization, and the erosion of national pride weakened Britain's foundation. America, too, now faces deepening political division, growing inequality, and an overreliance on foreign labor issues that echo the last days of the British Empire.

The Ottoman Empire, once a formidable military power, entered a period of decline during its "Tulip Era" a time marked by cultural excess, artistic indulgence, and an apathy toward governance. Like America today, Ottoman society became consumed by leisure, luxury, and superficiality. As younger generations lost the sense of purpose and drive that had once fueled the empire's expansion, internal weaknesses grew until the Ottoman Empire ultimately collapsed.

DECLINE OF SUCCESSIVE AMERICAN GENERATIONS

The decline of American values has unfolded gradually across generations, each contributing in its own way to the erosion of the principles that once made the nation great.

The Greatest Generation, known for their resilience and sacrifice during the Great Depression and World War II, built modern America through grit and determination. But as they laid the foundation for postwar prosperity, their hard-won success also paved the way for future generations to seek comfort over sacrifice.

The Baby Boomers and Generation X inherited the fruits of their parents' labor, fostering significant economic growth and social progress. Yet, they also laid the foundation for today's culture of entitlement and dependency. As consumerism became central to American life, subsequent generations became increasingly focused on individual comfort, leading to the gradual erosion of collective responsibility.

For Millennials and Generation Z, the world of affluence and instant gratification they have grown up in has fundamentally shaped their worldview. Their growing embrace of socialist ideals surveys show a significant percentage support government provided solutions reflects the broader cultural shift away from self-reliance and toward dependence. This mindset is symptomatic of a deeper cultural decline that prioritizes comfort and security over hard work and resilience.

A CALL FOR RENEWAL

As America teeters on the edge of collapse, the lessons of history have never been more relevant. The patterns of past empires are too familiar to ignore, and America now stands firmly in the Age of Decadence. The complacency, entitlement, and reliance on government support that defines modern American society threaten to destroy what previous generations built through sacrifice and perseverance.

But history also provides a way forward. If America is to avoid the fate of Rome, Britain, and the Ottomans, it must reject the allure of comfort and restore the values that once made it great: discipline, accountability, and hard work. This book will explore how America can break free from this cycle of decline. By holding Generation Z accountable, while equipping them with the tools they need to rebuild a sense of purpose and civic responsibility, we can restore the nation's prosperity and character.

The time for complacency is over. America's future depends on decisive action, and the stakes have never been higher.

DEFINING THE GENERATIONS

America's generational evolution tells a complex story of resilience, growth, and eventual decline. Each generation has played a distinct role in shaping the nation's trajectory, contributing to both its success and its gradual unraveling. By examining these generational shifts through the lens of Sir John Glubb's theory of civilizational rise and fall, we can see a clear pattern: a gradual movement from the values of hard work and collective sacrifice to a preoccupation with comfort, entitlement, and fragility.

THE GREATEST GENERATION

The Greatest Generation, born between 1901 and 1927, stands as a towering example of perseverance and unity. Having survived the Great Depression and led the country through World War II, they defined what it meant to sacrifice for the greater good. Their unwavering sense of duty to country and community became the bedrock of American strength during the mid20th century. This generation fits squarely into Glubb's "Age of Pioneers" and "Age of Conquests," where the values of determination, discipline, and moral responsibility prevailed. However, their rigid adherence to traditional values also meant they were slow to adapt to the social changes of their time, particularly in areas like race and gender equality. While they built the institutions that propelled

America's rise, they also laid the groundwork for future generations to grapple with unresolved societal inequalities.

THE SILENT GENERATION

Following in their footsteps, the Silent Generation, born between 1928 and 1945 carried forward many of the strengths of their predecessors. Known for their pragmatism and loyalty, they contributed to America's postwar prosperity, guiding the nation through a period of economic growth. Yet, unlike the generations that followed, they largely refrained from pushing for radical social reform. Their focus on stability and gradual change made them cautious when bold actions were needed. This reluctance to challenge authority left unresolved the structural issues of race and gender discrimination, which would erupt in the coming decades. The Silent Generation helped to maintain the economic prosperity of the "Age of Commerce," but their reticence to engage deeply with social issues left future generations with unfinished business.

BABY BOOMERS

The Baby Boomers, born between 1946 and 1964, came of age during a time of unparalleled optimism. They were the beneficiaries of the economic boom their parents helped create and played a pivotal role in shaping modern America. They led major social movements, civil rights, feminism, and environmentalism that radically transformed the cultural and political landscape. In Glubb's framework, they thrived in the "Age of Affluence," where abundance fueled not only economic growth but also the push for social progress. However, this generation also laid the foundation for the materialism and consumerism that have since dominated American life. As they aged, many Boomers shifted from activism to comfort seeking, contributing to a culture increasingly focused on individual gratification over collective responsibility. Their legacy is mixed: while they expanded freedom and opportunity for many, they also fostered a culture of excess that would weaken the values of self-reliance and sacrifice.

GEN X

Generation X, born between 1965 and 1980, was shaped by a period of social upheaval and economic uncertainty. Often referred to as the "latchkey" generation, many grew up in dual income or single parent households, which forced them to become independent and resourceful from an early age. This independence made Gen Xers adaptable, and their skepticism of authority encouraged innovation, particularly in the tech sector. They were the pioneers of the digital revolution, fundamentally changing how society operates. However, their deep-seated skepticism also led to political disengagement. Unlike the Baby Boomers, many Gen Xers remained outside of major social and political movements, prioritizing individualism over collective action. This detachment limited their impact on broader societal reforms, allowing political polarization and economic inequality to worsen.

MILLENNIALS

Millennials, born between 1981 and 1996, represent the first generation raised in a fully digital world. Their relationship with technology has profoundly shaped their worldview. On the one hand, Millennials have been key drivers of social change, advocating for inclusivity, diversity, and environmental awareness. They have leveraged technology to amplify their activism, mobilizing global movements with unprecedented speed. Millennials, however, have been criticized for their sense of entitlement and dependence on external validation, particularly through social media. Many experienced "helicopter parenting," which delayed their transition to independence, and as a result, a significant portion of Millennials remain financially and emotionally reliant on their parents well into adulthood. This overreliance has contributed to the perception that Millennials lack the resilience and self-sufficiency of previous generations. Their embrace of technology has been both a blessing and a curse, enabling them to drive change but also fostering a culture of instant gratification and superficial connection.

GEN Z

Generation Z, born between 1997 and 2012, is often described as the most tech savvy and socially conscious generation to date. They have grown up fully immersed in the digital age, which has made them highly informed and globally aware. Gen Z has been at the forefront of movements for social justice, climate action, and inclusivity. Their willingness to tackle systemic issues head-on is commendable, and their commitment to addressing the urgent challenges of our time, particularly climate change cannot be overstated. However, their heavy reliance on technology has also created significant challenges. Social media, while a powerful tool for activism, has fostered a culture of instant gratification, emotional fragility, and entitlement. Gen Z's embrace of "cancel culture" reveals their reluctance to engage in productive dialogue with differing opinions. This tendency has further polarized public discourse and made it difficult to foster the resilience and problem-solving skills necessary to navigate complex challenges.

Despite these criticisms, it is important to recognize that Gen Z's focus on social justice and environmental sustainability represents a significant positive shift. They are perhaps the most morally urgent generation in recent history, and their passion for creating a more equitable world stands in contrast to the individualism of previous generations.

However, their emotional fragility and dependence on technology reveal deeper societal issues that could hinder their ability to sustain the very movements they champion.

Looking at the broader generational arc, we can see a clear shift from resilience to fragility. The Greatest Generation thrived on sacrifice, building America's power and influence through sheer determination. As we move through the generations, however, this sense of resilience weakens. Baby Boomers, while activists in their youth, later contributed to the culture of comfort and entitlement that has since become dominant. Generation X, with its focus on individualism and disengagement, allowed political and social fragmentation to take root. Millennials, though passionate about inclusivity and equality, have struggled with independence and resilience, while Gen Z faces the unique challenge of balancing their digital activism with the need for emotional strength and open dialogue.

The gradual erosion of these foundational values sacrifice, discipline, and accountability accelerated with each generation. As Sir John Glubb's model of civilizational decline suggests, societies fall into the trap of abundance and comfort inevitably face decay. America is now at a critical juncture, with the entitlement and fragility of younger generations representing the culmination of this longstanding trend. Yet, this is not a narrative of inevitable collapse. The future depends on whether we can reinvigorate the values of hard work, civic responsibility, and resilience that once defined American greatness.

Each generation has both contributed to and reflected the broader societal shifts that have brought us to this moment. The question is whether we can reverse this trend before it is too late. To do so, we must look critically at how entitlement, comfort, and dependency have eroded the foundations of our society, and we must take bold, decisive action to restore the values that built this nation. The stakes are high, and the time for complacency is over. America's future depends on it.

CHAPTER ONE

A HISTORICAL LOOK AT SUCCESS AND DECLINE

The story of American society is inseparably linked to its generations. Each new cohort brings its values, triumphs, and flaws, contributing to the broader narrative of national progress or decline. By examining these generational shifts, we can trace a distinct evolution—one that moves from resilience and hard work to a present-day focus on comfort, entitlement, and fragility. However, this pattern is not unique to modern times. Throughout history, each generation has faced criticisms in its youth, only to emerge later as a powerful force for change. The generational transitions described by Sir John Glubb's "civilizational cycles" serve as a framework to understand the rise and fall of societal resilience.

THE GREATEST GENERATION (BORN 1901–1927)

The Greatest Generation, celebrated for its resilience during the Great Depression and World War II, is often lauded for its sacrifices and collective duty. Their contributions to America's postwar prosperity cannot be overstated. They were the pioneers and conquerors of their time, embodying the early stages of Glubb's model. This generation laid the foundations for American economic and military strength, fueled by a sense of duty and moral responsibility.

While revered for their contributions, the Greatest Generation also faced significant criticism in their youth. In the 1920s, they were often seen as reckless and self-indulgent, much like today's younger generations. The so-called "Roaring Twenties" were marked by hedonism, jazz culture, and a loosening of moral codes. Yet, when the nation was thrust into crisis, they showed their ability to adapt, sacrifice, and lead— proving that early critiques of their character were premature.

This is an important historical parallel: today's younger generations may similarly face critiques of fragility, but that does not prevent them from rising to meet future challenges. The Greatest Generation's transformation from a seemingly carefree youth to a generation defined by resilience highlights the potential for societal renewal in the face of adversity.

THE SILENT GENERATION (BORN 1928–1945)

The Silent Generation played a vital but understated role in America's postwar recovery, known for their pragmatism and discipline. They stabilized the economy after World War II and fostered an era of commercial growth. However, their political and social passivity, born of the caution instilled during the Great Depression and the war years, also had its drawbacks. Their reluctance to challenge authority allowed entrenched inequalities to persist, especially in terms of civil rights and gender equity.

But again, this generation faced criticisms in their early years. They were often viewed as too passive, too conformist. This critique mirrors some of the contemporary concerns about Millennials and Gen Z, who are often seen as more likely to protest on social media than engage in substantive reform. Yet, like their predecessors, the Silent Generation eventually played a crucial role in maintaining social stability and supporting the economic boom that their more rebellious children — the Baby Boomers — would inherit.

BABY BOOMERS (BORN 1946–1964)

Baby Boomers are perhaps the most paradoxical of all modern American generations. On one hand, they were champions of civil rights, feminism, and environmentalism. They led the movements that reshaped American society in the 1960s and 1970s. They later shifted focus to material comfort and consumerism, embodying the "Age of Affluence" in Glubb's cycle.

In their youth, Baby Boomers were often dismissed by their elders as overly idealistic, self-centered, and unwilling to conform to traditional societal values. Yet, their activism undeniably transformed America. This is a critical reminder that youthful idealism, often dismissed in the moment, can lead to profound cultural shifts.

However, their turn toward material excess and entitlement in later years has contributed to many of the issues facing younger generations today. By fostering a culture of consumerism, Baby Boomers passed on both the benefits of affluence and the burden of entitlement to future generations.

GENERATION X (BORN 1965–1980)

Generation X, often referred to as the "middle child" of modern generations, developed a deep sense of independence and adaptability. They were the first to grow up during widespread social upheaval, from the rise of dual income households to an increase in divorce rates, and this generation's skepticism of authority grew alongside these trends.

While their contributions to the tech revolution are significant, Generation X has been criticized for its political disengagement. They have often remained on the sidelines, choosing individualism over collective action. This detachment, while contributing to their reputation for independence, also meant that they failed to address the growing societal fragmentation and polarization that emerged during their adulthood.

Yet, like previous generations, Gen X faced their share of critique in their youth. Known as "slackers" and viewed as cynical, they were lacking the work ethic and social commitment of their parents. Despite this, they were pivotal in driving the digital revolution and creating the modern, technology driven world we inhabit today, proving that early judgments about a generation's potential can be misleading.

MILLENNIALS (BORN 1981–1996)

Millennials are often celebrated for their social activism, creativity, and digital savvy. They've driven movements for racial justice, LGBTQ+ rights, and environmental action. However, they have also been criticized for their reliance on external validation and a sense of entitlement, often blamed on "helicopter parenting" and the rise of social media.

It's important to note that the challenges facing Millennials are deeply rooted in larger economic and cultural shifts. They came of age during the 2008 financial crisis and have been saddled with unprecedented student debt and rising housing costs. In a 2018 Pew Research Center study, 62% of Millennials reported they were more financially burdened than previous generations at their age. Despite their push for inclusiveness and social reform, these economic pressures have delayed their independence, contributing to the perception of entitlement.

However, personal stories often reveal the resilience that exists beneath these surface critiques. Take the story of "John", a Millennial who, after losing his job during the financial crisis, pivoted himself to start his own social enterprise focused on environmental sustainability. John's journey from financial insecurity to entrepreneurship illustrates the potential for Millennials to leverage their unique challenges into opportunities for meaningful change.

GENERATION Z (BORN 1997–2012)

As digital natives, Gen Z is arguably the most socially conscious generation in history. They have embraced movements for climate action, social justice, and inclusiveness, often using technology as their primary tool for activism. However, their reliance on technology has also contributed to emotional fragility and a culture of instant gratification. A 2019 study by the American Psychological Association found that 90% of Gen Z reported experiencing stress related to social media, and over half described themselves as "overwhelmed" by the pressures of online validation.

But just as previous generations overcame early criticisms, Gen Z has the potential to harness its activism and digital fluency for significant societal impact. A case in point is Greta Thunberg, a Gen Z climate activist who has become the face of a global movement. Thunberg's ability to channel her anxiety over climate change into effective activism provides a model for how Gen Z can overcome the fragility that technology has fostered.

A SHIFT FROM RESILIENCE TO FRAGILITY

From the Greatest Generation to Gen Z, we see clear patterns in Glubb's model of civilizational rise and decline. Each generation, once criticized for its perceived failings, eventually rose above them. The Greatest Generation, once seen as frivolous in their youth, became the epitome of resilience. The Baby Boomers, once idealists, became materialists. Millennials, while seen as entitled, have also spearheaded social and technological innovations that will shape the future.

Yet, as affluence has increased, the values of sacrifice and discipline have eroded. The challenge now is to learn from the past and reclaim the ethos of resilience, responsibility, and civic duty that earlier generations embodied. History shows that every generation faces adversity and criticism—but also that each can rise above it and contribute profoundly to society.

Without a return to the principles of hard work and collective responsibility, we risk following the same pattern of decline seen in civilizations throughout history. When societies forget the value of perseverance and dedication, they lose their innovative edge, their sense of purpose, and their resilience in the face of adversity. The decline is gradual but inevitable—what starts as a shift away from personal accountability becomes a societal norm of entitlement and complacency. Historical empires, from Rome to the Mayans, have shown us that once a culture embraces decadence and disconnection from a shared sense of duty, it spirals toward stagnation and collapse.

Hard work isn't merely about individual success; it's the engine that drives progress and strengthens the social fabric. Collective responsibility ensures that each person contributes meaningfully to the wellbeing of the community, fostering unity and shared goals. When these values diminish, the consequences aren't just economic; they are moral and cultural. The decay of these foundational values results in a society that prioritizes short-term comfort over long-term stability, and that sacrifices the needs of the collective for the indulgences of the individual.

To avoid this fate, we must look to our history and recognize that the survival and prosperity of a civilization rest on the shoulders of people who will work not only for themselves but for something greater. It's only through commitment, grit, and the recognition of our interconnectedness that we can hope to build a sustainable future. The lessons of the past are clear: without hard work and collective responsibility, the road ahead leads to fragmentation, disillusionment, and ultimately, decline.

CHAPTER TWO

THE ENTITLEMENT EPIDEMIC

American progress today is increasingly defined by the pursuit of individual comfort rather than chasing collective responsibility and perseverance. This shift is not accidental; it is the product of a cultural pivot towards instant gratification. In a world where speed and convenience have become the highest ideals, patience and diligence—the traits that once formed the backbone of American progress—are fading into the background. The entitlement mindset that has emerged is not a natural evolution, but a byproduct of a world shaped by powerful forces like technology, consumerism, and evolving political ideologies that place more emphasis on government intervention than on personal accountability.

Technology has made life easier in countless ways, but it has also fostered a growing expectation that everything we want should be available at the push of a button, with no effort required. Social media bombards us with curated images of perfect lives, where success appears instantaneously, and struggle is hidden from view. This fuels a dangerous belief that comfort is a right, not a reward for effort. The proliferation of on demand services—from streaming entertainment to next day deliveries—conditions us to expect satisfaction now, and with as little work as possible. The value of perseverance has eroded, replaced by the allure of shortcuts and quick fixes.

Consumerism has compounded this problem, feeding into a culture where worth is measured by what we own rather than what we contribute. Advertisements promise happiness through products, selling us the idea that our problems can be solved through consumption. This relentless focus on personal acquisition encourages a "me first" attitude, which further distances us from any sense of community or collective responsibility. The result is a society where people feel entitled not only to material goods but also to success without sacrifice, where the line between need and desire is blurred beyond recognition.

Political ideologies have also played a role in this shift. Increasing emphasis on government intervention has, many times, fostered a dependent mindset that erodes personal accountability. Safety nets, while crucial for supporting those in genuine need, have sometimes transformed into systems that disincentivize individual effort. The idea of pulling oneself up by the bootstraps, once celebrated as the essence of the

American spirit, is now often dismissed as unrealistic or outdated. This ideological shift implies that the government should ensure everyone's comfort, removing the individual's role in their own success.

The consequences of this entitlement epidemic are profound. If left unchecked, it risks stunting not only individual potential but also the broader growth of society. When people believe they deserve rewards without effort, innovation stagnates. Creativity and resilience—qualities that flourish under adversity and drive societal advancement in the face of guaranteed comfort. We lose the incentive to push boundaries, solve problems, or engage meaningfully with the challenges we face. Instead of striving for greatness, we settle for mere adequacy, if someone else will do the hard work required to keep society.

This shift threatens the core of what once made American progress so remarkable: the belief that through hard work, perseverance, and a sense of duty to something larger than oneself, anyone could rise above their circumstances. By emphasizing individual comfort over collective achievement, we risk becoming a society that no longer dreams big or reaches high. The cost is not just the loss of personal potential but also the erosion of a shared vision for a better future—one built on the strength, sacrifice, and contributions of all.

To reverse this course, we need to reembrace the values of perseverance and responsibility. It is imperative to foster a culture where individuals understand that true fulfillment comes not from instant comfort but from the satisfaction of working towards something meaningful, both for themselves and for their community. Only by doing so can we hope to restore a sense of purpose that transcends the shallow allure of entitlement, enabling both individuals and society to thrive once more.

THE ENTITLEMENT EPIDEMIC: A CULTURE OF INSTANT GRATIFICATION

Generation Z has grown up in an environment where convenience is king and immediate gratification is the norm. Whether it's the ability to order food online and have it delivered within minutes, or gaining instant fame on platforms like TikTok, the modern world provides countless examples of how quickly desires can be met with minimal effort. This reliance on instant rewards has deeply influenced how Gen Z navigates success and achievement. The result is a generation that is often more focused on receiving praise and benefits in the short term rather than putting in the sustained effort required for long-term success.

The digital world has played a pivotal role in fostering this mentality. Social media platforms like TikTok offer young people a chance at viral fame with little more than a few seconds of content. Unlike previous generations, who often had to spend years building careers in media or entertainment, today's Gen Zers can become household names overnight. The ease with which success can be achieved on these platforms has fed into a broader sense of entitlement, where individuals come to expect instant recognition without investing in the skills or effort that were once seen as prerequisites for success.

VIRAL FAME THROUGH TIKTOK AND SOCIAL MEDIA

Perhaps the most visible example of this entitlement mentality is the rise of viral fame on social media platforms. A single video on TikTok can catapult an individual to stardom, amassing millions of followers and lucrative sponsorship deals without the individual developing any enduring skills. The Guardian's research shows that young TikTok users, starting from 16 years old, can achieve rapid success through viral content, gaining financial gain and social influence.

This phenomenon contrasts with previous generations' paths to success in entertainment and media, which emphasized hard work and resilience. Today, fleeting popularity has replaced the years of practice and perseverance that once defined success, reinforcing the notion that rapid achievement is not only possible but deserved. This mindset permeates far beyond social media, influencing how Generation Z approaches education, work, and personal growth.

JOBHOPPING FOR QUICK PROMOTIONS

Many young workers expect quick career advancement and better benefits without the experience or commitment. Studies by Gallup reveal that nearly 21% of Millennials and Gen Z workers change jobs annually, driven by dissatisfaction with the perceived lack of immediate upward mobility. This contrasts with the values of earlier generations, who typically prized job loyalty and saw gradual career progression as a natural part of working life.

The desire for rapid promotions and benefits without proving one's value has become a defining characteristic of Gen Z's relationship with work. Many times, young workers enter roles expecting they should be rewarded almost immediately, regardless of the time spent mastering their craft. Workplace perks like flexible hours and free meals, popularized by tech startups, exacerbate impatience with traditional career trajectories. While these benefits can be valuable, they have also fueled unrealistic expectations about work and the rewards that come with it.

Data from LinkedIn highlights how these changing expectations manifest in practice. The average tenure of a Gen Z employee is just over two years, a dramatic contrast to the six-year average tenure seen among Baby Boomers. Job-hopping reflects entitlement to fast career growth, contributing to a generational shift away from patience and long-term contribution.

RISING WORKPLACE EXPECTATIONS: FLEXIBILITY AND BENEFITS WITHOUT PROVEN VALUE

The entitlement mindset in the workplace goes beyond promotions and salary expectations. Many Gen Z employees also expect workplace flexibility and a host of benefits from the outset, often without demonstrating the value they bring to their employers. A Deloitte study reveals that over 75% of Gen Z workers consider workplace flexibility a top priority, with expectations for remote work, adjustable hours, and generous paid time off. These demands pose challenges for employers, especially in entry-level positions where in person collaboration and structured learning are vital for skill development.

The demand for such privileges early in one's career signals a shift in how young workers view employment. Where previous generations saw these benefits as something to be earned after demonstrating long-term commitment and contribution, many Gen Z employees now see them as entitlements from day one. This expectation puts employers in a difficult position balancing the need to attract young talent while ensuring that performance-based incentives remain central to workplace culture.

The entitlement mindset also extends to more traditional benefits like healthcare packages, bonuses, and even equity stakes in companies. Many Gen Z workers expect these rewards immediately upon being hired, regardless of their contribution to the company's success. Young workers' expectations clash with employers' ability to meet them, highlighting a cultural shift towards entitlement.

CONNECTION TO SOCIALIST AND LIBERAL IDEALS: REINFORCING DEPENDENCY

The entitlement epidemic does not exist in isolation; it is deeply connected to broader political and social ideologies that have gained traction in recent decades, particularly socialist and liberal ideals that emphasize government assistance and societal safety nets. While these ideologies often serve the noble purpose of protecting vulnerable populations, they have also contributed to a culture where dependency is normalized, and personal responsibility is increasingly sidelined.

At the heart of these political movements is the belief that basic needs such as healthcare, housing, and education should be guaranteed by the government, often without corresponding individual contribution. It is important for addressing inequalities and providing a safety net but may foster a dependency mindset. Cato Institute research suggests that increased government support can lower workforce participation rates.

Among younger generations, particularly Gen Z, there is a growing expectation that government support should be readily available, with fewer strings attached. This shift reflects a deeper cultural trend where individual effort and self-reliance are no longer seen as paramount, and where entitlement to external support takes precedence over personal contribution.

THE DECLINE OF PERSONAL RESPONSIBILITY

The erosion of personal responsibility is perhaps the most concerning aspect of the entitlement epidemic. As liberal ideals emphasize wealth redistribution and government intervention, the traditional connection between hard work and reward has weakened. In this environment, individuals are more likely to develop an attitude that success and financial security are owed to them, rather than something to be earned through effort and perseverance. This mindset not only undermines personal growth but also has broader societal implications, as fewer people are motivated to innovate, take risks, or contribute to the collective good.

When personal responsibility is minimized, individuals are less likely to develop the skills necessary to navigate life's challenges. Resilience, discipline, and the ability to overcome adversity qualities that once defined American success are increasingly overshadowed by a reliance on external forces to solve personal problems. This shift has significant consequences for both individual wellbeing and societal productivity, as fewer people will engage in the hard work required to achieve lasting success.

THE RISK OF STUNTED GROWTH

The entitlement epidemic is not just a social irritant, it is a fundamental threat to the fabric of our society. At its core, entitlement creates an expectation that rewards are inherent rather than earned. This mindset, when adopted at scale, leads to a stagnation of ambition, a waning desire to contribute, and an erosion of the collective work ethic that once defined American society. The consequences of such an epidemic go far beyond personal stagnation; they risk grinding the wheels of progress to a halt.

When individuals expect rewards without corresponding effort, the entire foundation of innovation and prosperity crumbles. The concept of pushing boundaries, of persevering through failure, and ultimately, the ability to create meaningful change all hinge on the notion that reward follows sacrifice. Entitlement undermines this principle. It removes the hunger for success and replaces it with a complacency that suffocates creativity and resilience. The incentive to innovate vanishes when the fruits of innovation are promised without the journey of growth, struggle, and eventual triumph.

The impact on society is profound. The very dynamism that has fueled American progress for centuries is at risk. Our ability to adapt, to face challenges with courage, and to create solutions for increasingly complex problems is directly tied to the values of personal responsibility, merit, and perseverance. Entitlement weakens this connection, fostering a culture where people expect to receive more while doing less. The ripple effects are seen across our educational institutions, workplaces, and communities, where effort and excellence are no longer universally respected or incentivized.

The result? A less productive, less inventive, and ultimately less competitive society. Our ability to solve our greatest challenges, whether they are economic, technological, or social, relies on individuals willing to invest effort without the guarantee of immediate reward. But when entitlement takes root, the drive to persevere, to take risks, and to push beyond the status quo fades. A culture of entitlement breeds dependency, and dependency fosters a populace that is unable or unwilling to meet the demands of a complex and changing world.

If we are to reverse this trend, a cultural shift is imperative. We must refocus on the values that have historically underpinned personal and societal growth: delayed gratification, personal accountability, and a relentless commitment to long-term progress. These values are not mere ideals, they are the bedrock upon which innovation, growth, and resilience are built. A return to emphasizing these virtues is crucial not only for individual success but for ensuring that society remains vibrant, capable, and forward-thinking.

Without such a shift, the trend toward dependency and entitlement will only deepen, eroding the very essence of what has made America a beacon of possibility. The future of American society hinges on our ability to nurture a culture that values effort, celebrates sacrifice, and understands that meaningful rewards are earned, not given. This is not just a call for change; it is a necessity if we are to reclaim the dynamism and resolve that has always driven our nation forward.

ESCAPING THE ENTITLEMENT TRAP

Breaking free from the entitlement epidemic requires us to reembrace the values that once defined American progress—delayed gratification, hard work, and personal responsibility. These qualities were not only cornerstones of individual success but were also the driving force behind the nation's greatest achievements, from economic growth to societal innovation. Yet, in recent decades, the emphasis has shifted away from these foundational values towards an unhealthy focus on comfort and immediacy. Social media, evolving workplace trends, and shifting political ideologies have all contributed to this entitlement mindset, but the solution lies in reclaiming the principles of resilience and accountability that propelled us forward in the past.

Social media, while connecting us in unprecedented ways, has also fueled unrealistic expectations about success. Platforms are flooded with curated snapshots of perfect lives — instant success stories that conceal the years of effort behind the scenes. The constant bombardment of polished, effortless achievements distorts our perception of reality, making it harder to appreciate the value of struggle and perseverance. We have been led to believe that success should come quickly and easily, without the years of learning, failing, and trying again that true growth requires. Reclaiming delayed gratification means understanding that meaningful accomplishments take time, and that the path is often filled with setbacks and moments of uncertainty.

In the workplace, the trend towards prioritizing convenience over challenge has further contributed to the entitlement culture. The rise of remote work, the push for balance of work-life, and the focus on employee comfort are all positive developments in moderation. However, when taken to extremes, they can foster environments where resilience and adaptability are undervalued. The ability to tackle onerous tasks, endure pressure, and push beyond comfort zones are essential skills that drive personal and professional growth. By celebrating effort over ease, we can reestablish a culture that respects not just achieving results, but the process that it takes to get there — the grind, the setbacks, and the eventual victories that come from hard work.

Political ideologies have also played a pivotal role in shaping the current climate of entitlement. As the discourse has shifted towards emphasizing government intervention, there has been a corresponding decline in the emphasis on personal accountability. While social safety nets are crucial for supporting vulnerable populations, they must be carefully balanced to ensure they do not unintentionally disincentivize personal effort or foster dependency. It's time for a cultural shift that encourages individuals to take responsibility for their own lives, while also supporting those who genuinely need help to get back on their feet. The key lies in promoting policies that empower people to become self-sufficient, rather than fostering reliance on external systems for basic survival.

To successfully combat the entitlement epidemic, we must spark a collective cultural shift that celebrates perseverance, long-term skill development, and individual growth. Society needs to start rewarding the slow and often uncomfortable journey of learning, developing expertise, and building character. We must encourage an appreciation for those who work tirelessly to acquire mastery, even if their progress is not immediately visible. Success is not about the flashy, momentary recognition that fades as quickly as it comes — it is about the steady, consistent pursuit of excellence that builds true competence and confidence.

In education, for instance, this means teaching children that failure is not something to be feared or avoided, but a vital part of the learning process. It's about showing young people that the most worthwhile achievements are those that require persistence and resilience. In our communities, it means celebrating stories of individuals who have overcome hardship through determination and grit, rather than focusing solely on those who appear to have achieved success effortlessly. And in our workplaces, it means fostering an environment that values ongoing growth and development over quick wins.

Without this shift, we risk continuing down a dangerous path where dependency and complacency become the defining characteristics of our society. The entitlement mindset leads people to expect rewards without effort, to shy away from challenges, and to avoid taking responsibility for their actions. This cycle of dependency weakens both individuals and the collective fabric of our nation. A society that does not value hard work, personal accountability, and resilience will inevitably become fragile—unable to adapt, unable to innovate, and ultimately unable to sustain itself in the face of challenges.

Breaking free from the entitlement epidemic is not just about changing individual attitudes; it is about transforming the very culture we live in. It requires us to refocus on the principles that lead to real growth and progress—both for ourselves and for society. By embracing the values of delayed gratification, hard work, and personal responsibility, we can reclaim a future where individuals strive for greatness, not because it is easy, but because it is worth it. Only then can we hope to build a society that is resilient, innovative, and capable of overcoming the challenges of tomorrow.

CHAPTER THREE

WOKENESS AND CANCEL CULTURE

In recent years, the concept of "wokeness" has undergone a dramatic transformation. What began as a genuine call for social justice, rooted in empathy and the pursuit of equality, has gradually morphed into something far more complex and contentious—a tool for enforcing ideological conformity. Initially, the movement was focused on addressing legitimate grievances, such as systemic racism, gender inequality, and other forms of social injustice. It gave voice to marginalized groups and highlighted issues that had been overlooked for far too long. However, as its influence grew, wokeness evolved into a rigid ideology, one that increasingly stifles free speech and undermines the very principles of open dialogue and debate that are crucial for a healthy society.

The early days of wokeness were characterized by a spirit of awareness and accountability, a desire to bring attention to injustices that were too often swept under the rug. It was about waking up to the realities of discrimination and inequity and urging others to do the same. But over time, the movement has shifted. It has become less about awareness and more about adherence to a prescribed set of beliefs. Instead of encouraging diverse perspectives and constructive debate, wokeness demands strict conformity. Those who question or deviate from the accepted narrative risk being ostracized, silenced, or even "canceled" a term that symbolizes the most extreme consequence of stepping out of line.

Generation Z, born into an era of rapid social change and digital interconnectedness, has found itself at the forefront of this transformation. They are the first generation to fully grow up with social media, a powerful tool that has amplified both the reach and the impact of wokeness. Platforms like Twitter, TikTok, and Instagram have become battlegrounds where cultural norms are constantly being defined, contested, and enforced. Cancel culture, a visible manifestation of this shift, has emerged as a tool for punishing those who do not conform. It operates with a speed and intensity that is unprecedented, fueled by viral outrage and an expectation of moral purity that leaves little room for nuance or forgiveness.

The idea of holding people accountable for their words and actions is not inherently wrong—after all, accountability is a fundamental component of justice. However, cancel culture often goes beyond accountability, veering into the territory of public shaming and character assassination. It is not just about addressing wrongdoing; it is about erasing individuals from the public sphere altogether. The consequences can be severe, careers destroyed, reputations shattered, and lives upended, all in the name of enforcing a particular vision of social justice. The result is a chilling effect on free speech, where people become afraid to express their opinions or ask questions for fear of backlash. Instead of fostering a culture of learning and growth, cancel culture fosters fear and conformity, stifling the very discourse that is necessary for progress.

This chapter explores the origins and evolution of wokeness, tracing its path from a well-intentioned movement for social awareness to its current form as a tool of ideological enforcement. We delve into the factors that have driven this shift, including the influence of social media, the rise of identity politics, and the increasing polarization of public discourse. By examining the cultural dynamics that have shaped wokeness, we can better understand how a movement that started with such promise has become so divisive.

The impact of cancel culture on society is complex, and its effects are far-reaching. Through a series of case studies, this chapter will highlight the real-world consequences of cancel culture—both for the individuals targeted and for the broader society. We will look at instances where public figures have been "canceled" for past mistakes, often with little regard for context or the possibility of redemption. These case studies will illustrate the dangers of an unforgiving culture, where people are not allowed to grow or change, and where the line between accountability and persecution becomes dangerously blurred.

Ultimately, the evolution of wokeness and the rise of cancel culture raise important questions about the kind of society we want to build. Are we fostering an environment where people feel empowered to speak up and engage in meaningful dialogue, or are we creating a climate of fear where only those who conform are allowed a voice? This chapter argues that to move forward, we must find a balanced one that allows us to address injustice without resorting to ideological tyranny, one that values free speech and open dialogue as essential components of a just society.

If we are to overcome the divisiveness that characterizes our current cultural moment, we must reclaim the original spirit of wokeness—a spirit that is about awareness, empathy, and the pursuit of justice, not about enforcing conformity or silencing dissent. True progress comes not from shutting down voices we disagree with, but from engaging with them, understanding them, and, when necessary, challenging them in constructive ways. Only by doing so can we hope to create a society that is both just and free—one where people are encouraged to grow, to learn, and to contribute to the collective good without fear of being erased for their imperfections.

THE RISE OF WOKENESS: FROM SOCIAL JUSTICE TO THOUGHT POLICING

The term "wokeness" originally referred to an enlightened awareness of social injustices, particularly those faced by marginalized communities. In its early form, wokeness was a powerful tool for fostering inclusivity and empathy, bringing greater awareness to issues like racial inequality, gender discrimination, and social inequity. For a time, wokeness played a crucial role in reshaping societal attitudes, encouraging people to confront uncomfortable truths and work towards a more just and equal society.

However, over time, wokeness has evolved into something more rigid. It has transitioned from a movement centered on advocacy and inclusivity to one that often enforces ideological purity and moral certainty. Today, wokeness is frequently used as a weapon to shut down dissent and stifle debate, particularly on social media platforms where discussions quickly escalate into moral outrage. Cancel culture, a byproduct of this shift, has become the primary method for policing thought, punishing individuals, businesses, or public figures who are perceived to have violated social norms, regardless of the context or severity of the offense.

THE EVOLUTION OF WOKENESS

The transformation of wokeness from a tool of social justice to one of thought policing is most evident in the rise of cancel culture. What started as a legitimate effort to hold individuals and institutions accountable for harmful behaviors has, many times, devolved into a form of ideological enforcement. Cancel culture is now characterized by swift, often disproportionate punishment for perceived transgressions, leaving little room for nuance, discussion, or redemption.

Sociological research from The Brookings Institution highlights how cancel culture flourishes in environments where moral absolutism dominates, replacing thoughtful debate with rigid expectations of conformity. This shift is noticeable on social media, where outrage can be amplified at an alarming rate, and public judgment is rendered without due process. In this climate, mistakes, whether they occurred years ago or were taken out of context, are often met with immediate condemnation, leaving the accused with few avenues for defense or reconciliation.

THE PSYCHOLOGICAL ROOTS OF CANCEL CULTURE

The psychological drivers behind cancel culture are complex but can be traced, in part, to moral absolutism the belief that one's views on social issues are not just correct but the only morally acceptable ones. This mindset has created an environment where dissenting voices are not seen as opportunities for dialogue but as existential threats to be eradicated. Once someone or something is labeled as morally wrong, there is little room for rehabilitation or discussion. The result is an ideological battleground where opposing perspectives are dismissed outright rather than considered.

Social media has amplified this phenomenon, creating echo chambers where groupthink and moral certainty reign supreme. Social media platforms like Twitter and Facebook are battlegrounds for enforcing ideological purity, with viral posts leading to widespread shaming. The fast and intense responses create a chilling effect on expressing controversial opinions.

Psychological studies suggest environments characterized by high levels of social pressure—such as those fostered by cancel culture—suppress genuine expression and encourage conformity. When individuals perceive that deviating from the dominant narrative may lead to harsh social consequences, such as public shaming or ostracization, they become likely to self-censor. The instinct to avoid conflict or protect one's reputation often leads to the silencing of personal viewpoints, even if those perspectives might contribute valuable insight or promote meaningful dialogue. The result is a chilling effect where authentic debate and diverse opinions are systematically driven underground, leaving only a narrow band of "acceptable" ideas that can be voiced without fear of repercussions.

Stifling intellectual diversity under such conditions creates a vicious cycle. When individuals feel pressured to align their beliefs and public statements with the majority, even if those beliefs do not reflect their true thoughts, the appearance of consensus emerges. This illusion of unanimity only serves to intensify the social pressure, reinforcing the notion that the dominant narrative is not just the majority view, but the only morally or socially acceptable one. As a result, people become more hesitant to question or challenge that narrative, fearing that any deviation, no matter how slight or well-intentioned, will be met with a disproportionate backlash.

This cycle ultimately leads to an environment where only one acceptable narrative remains. The space for intellectual diversity, the hallmark of a healthy, thriving society — gradually shrinks, replaced by an echo chamber where dissent is not tolerated. Ideas are no longer evaluated on their merit, but on their alignment with prevailing views. The potential for constructive disagreement, which can lead to deeper understanding and progress, is lost. Instead of being a forum for exchange, the public sphere becomes a minefield, where individuals tread cautiously, constantly aware of the risk of stepping out of line.

The fear of public condemnation is a powerful force, capable of changing how people think, speak, and behave. The risk of being publicly shamed or "canceled" for voicing an unpopular or unconventional opinion acts as a deterrent to open dialogue. It discourages individuals from exploring ideas that may challenge the status quo, even if those ideas have the potential to spur growth and positive change. This suppression of free thought and expression not only affects those directly targeted by cancel culture but also sends a message to onlookers: stay silent, stay in line, or face the same fate.

In environments dominated by social pressure, the cost of honesty becomes too high for many people. Studies on group dynamics and social influence have long shown that when the fear of exclusion or criticism looms large, people will often choose conformity over authenticity. This behavior is rooted in a fundamental human need to belong, to be part of a community, and to avoid the discomfort of social conflict. However, when conformity is driven by fear rather than genuine agreement, the resulting "consensus" is fragile and devoid of genuine commitment. It is a superficial unity that crumbles under scrutiny because it is built not on shared beliefs but on a shared fear of punishment.

The implications of this are significant for society at large. When intellectual diversity is stifled, innovation suffers. Progress depends on the ability to question existing ideas, to propose alternatives, and to engage in rigorous debate. It requires a culture where people feel safe to think differently, to take risks, and to learn from failure. Cancel culture, by punishing deviation, creates an atmosphere where people are reluctant to take those risks. The fear of public condemnation limits creativity, as individuals become more concerned with avoiding controversy than with pursuing truth or excellence.

The suppression of dissenting voices can lead to a dangerous polarization, where those who disagree with the dominant narrative are pushed to the fringes, their grievances left unaddressed and their perspectives unheard. This exclusion can breed resentment, creating an undercurrent of discontent that further divides society. Instead of fostering understanding and unity, the environment of social pressure and ideological conformity leads to fragmentation, with people retreating into insular groups where their views are affirmed without challenge. The lack of open dialogue across different perspectives makes it even more difficult to bridge divides and find common ground.

Breaking this cycle requires a deliberate effort to foster environments where free speech and intellectual diversity are valued. It means encouraging a culture that welcomes different viewpoints, where people can disagree without fear of being vilified, and where the focus is on understanding and growth rather than punishment. True progress comes from the exchange of ideas—from the willingness to listen, to be challenged, and to evolve. Without this exchange, we risk becoming a society where conformity is prized over curiosity, where comfort is valued over truth, and where the fear of condemnation silences the very voices that could lead us to a better future.

CANCEL CULTURE IN ACTION: CASE STUDIES OF PUBLIC FIGURES

Cancel culture has become a highly visible and contentious phenomenon, impacting many public figures and ordinary individuals alike. When a high-profile person is "canceled," it's often because of statements or actions that are perceived as offensive, even if they were made years ago or taken out of context. The repercussions can be swift and overwhelming, leading to lost jobs, severed relationships, or even public shaming campaigns.

The issue here is that the consequences can be hugely disproportionate to the initial action or statement. One mistake can destroy a career without an opportunity for dialogue, growth, or redemption. This kind of environment breeds fear, stifles creativity, and discourages individuals from expressing unique perspectives, lest they become the next target of the mob.

This phenomenon also raises concerns about how we, as a society, handle conflict and disagreement. There's an argument to be made that cancel culture discourages learning and genuine understanding, opting instead for immediate judgment and social exile. By closing the door to conversations, we lose an opportunity for change, awareness, and mutual understanding.

CASE STUDY 1: COMEDIAN KEVIN HART

Kevin Hart's experience illustrates how past actions can have lasting repercussions in today's cancel culture climate. In 2019, Hart was selected to host the prestigious Academy Awards, a major milestone in his career that promised both recognition and a significant platform. However, this opportunity was abruptly stripped away after old tweets containing offensive jokes resurfaced. These tweets, originally posted years before, were crude attempts at humor that targeted the LGBTQ+ community, reflecting a time when societal norms around comedy and sensitivity were markedly different. Despite passaging time and the evolving cultural landscape, these old comments suddenly became frontpage news.

When the backlash began, Hart issued multiple public apologies. He expressed genuine remorse and explained how his views had changed significantly since he made those remarks. He spoke openly about personal growth, emphasizing that he no longer held the views expressed in those old tweets and that, as a person, he had matured. Hart's apologies were heartfelt and accompanied by public discussions about how he had become a more understanding and empathetic individual. Yet, the backlash remained swift and relentless. The Academy offered him an ultimatum: apologize again or step down as the host. Despite having already apologized, Hart resigned, citing his exhaustion with repeatedly apologizing for mistakes that he had sincerely sought to make amends for.

This incident underscores a key dynamic of cancel culture: even when individuals take responsibility for their past behavior and show genuine personal growth, the weight of historical infractions can prove too great to overcome. The reaction to Hart's old tweets was not merely about holding him accountable, it became an outright rejection of his ability to change. It was as if no amount of personal reflection, no evolution in his beliefs, could redeem him in the eyes of his critics. For many, that Hart had already apologized years earlier and had since made visible efforts to support marginalized communities was overshadowed by a demand for further public penance.

Hart's case highlights an uncomfortable truth about cancel culture: it often operates under the belief that past wrongdoings, regardless of how distant they are or how much an individual has grown since, deserve continuous punishment. There is a refusal to acknowledge that people are capable of change, that they can learn from their mistakes and make meaningful contributions to society despite their past. Cancel culture, in its most punitive form, does not prioritize growth or redemption; instead, it focuses on retribution and exclusion. The notion of "once guilty, always guilty" seems to dominate, leaving little room for nuance or understanding that people are complex and capable of evolving.

This approach is inherently problematic because it disregards the core human capacity for growth and change. By rejecting public apologies as inadequate and punishing individuals regardless of the steps they have taken towards positive change, cancel culture discourages genuine reflection and accountability. If no path to redemption is available—if sincere efforts to apologize and improve are always met with skepticism or outright rejection—then what incentive does anyone have to grow or to confront their past mistakes? In an environment where forgiveness is unattainable, accountability becomes an empty concept. People may become defensive rather than reflective, knowing that no amount of contrition will ever be deemed enough.

This punitive stance reinforces a cultural environment where the potential for change is overshadowed by the desire for retribution. It sends the message that past mistakes define an individual permanently, and that their future contributions are invalidated by their past transgressions, regardless of the distance they've traveled since. Instead of fostering a culture where people are encouraged to learn from their errors, admit their wrongs, and strive for improvement, cancel culture can create an atmosphere of fear. This fear leads to people hiding their imperfections rather than acknowledging them, making meaningful dialogue about personal growth nearly impossible.

Kevin Hart's experience is a stark reminder of the importance of balancing accountability with empathy. If we genuinely want to foster a society that values progress, we must be willing to accept that people can and do change. Holding individuals accountable for harmful actions is necessary, but that accountability should also involve recognizing their journey towards improvement. Cancel culture's tendency to demand absolute moral perfection creates unrealistic standards, and those who fall short— essentially everyone, at some point or another—face consequences that do not align with the broader goals of justice or understanding.

By examining cases like Hart's, it becomes evident that the culture of public shaming and perpetual punishment does more harm than good. It risks creating a society where people are unwilling to take risks or speak openly, out of fear that any misstep, no matter how far in the past, will result in irreversible consequences. Instead of encouraging growth, it fosters a climate of rigidity, where mistakes are not allowed, and personal history is weaponized.

True accountability should involve both acknowledging past wrongs and supporting the individual's efforts to do better. It should create opportunities for growth, not simply opportunities for punishment. Only by recognizing that people are more than the worst things they have ever said or done can we create an environment where real change is possible. If cancel culture continues to deny the possibility of redemption, it will not only stunt individual potential but will also inhibit societal growth, creating a landscape where fear of condemnation stifles innovation, creativity, and the human capacity for empathy and transformation.

CASE STUDY 2: PROFESSOR BRET WEINSTEIN

Bret Weinstein, a biology professor at Evergreen State College, found himself at the center of a major controversy in 2017 when he opposed the college's "Day of Absence" event. The Day of Absence, traditionally a voluntary event where people of color left campus to show their vital contributions to the community, underwent a significant change in 2017. The new iteration called for white students and faculty to leave campus instead, effectively reversing the original premise. Weinstein's objection wasn't rooted in a rejection of the event's underlying goal of fostering dialogue on race relations; he clarified that he fully supported the goal of addressing systemic inequalities and bridging racial divides. Rather, his disagreement lay in the method. He argued that mandating the exclusion of individuals based on their race was counterproductive to the very message of inclusion, mutual respect, and equality that the event sought to promote.

Weinstein's intent was to provoke a constructive discussion on how to best tackle issues of race, how to foster inclusivity without resorting to divisive methods that, in his view, mirrored the same exclusionary practices the event counteracted. He wished to highlight the danger of mandating any form of exclusion, which, regardless of intent, inherently undermines the principles of unity and commonality. Yet, instead of his stance igniting a thoughtful dialogue, it became the catalyst for widespread protests. Students and faculty alike accused him of being a racist, his words were twisted to imply he opposed progress, and he became a target of intense personal threats and vitriolic accusations. The situation escalated so much that Weinstein was eventually forced to resign, unable to continue in an environment that had become not only hostile but physically unsafe for him and his family.

Weinstein's case serves as a glaring example of how cancel culture has deeply infiltrated academic spaces, institutions that were once considered bastions of free thought, rigorous debate, and intellectual diversity. Evergreen State College, long known for its progressive values and emphasis on free inquiry, became a place intolerant of dissenting opinions. The severe consequences Weinstein faced directly resulted from the college's refusal to accommodate any deviation from the dominant narrative. The reaction to his objection was immediate and severe, characterized by a reflexive condemnation of his perceived noncompliance with the prevailing ideology. There was no effort to understand the nuance of his argument or to acknowledge his support for racial equality. Instead, the dialogue turned into a campaign to silence and vilify him, as if even questioning the method of pursuing justice equated to opposing justice itself.

This incident underscores a disturbing trend that has taken root in both academic and broader cultural spheres: questioning popular or dominant narratives, even from a place of genuine concern, increasingly leads to harsh backlash rather than productive engagement. The opposition to Weinstein's stance highlighted a broader issue of intolerance and fragility among the younger generation, a cohort that often champions ideals like inclusion and empathy while paradoxically showing little tolerance for viewpoints that deviate from their own. Weinstein, who sought only to point out the dangers of mandating racial exclusion to achieve equality, was branded a racist and effectively ostracized. The personal threats he faced, coupled with the hostile environment that developed on campus, were not just attacks on an individual, they were assaults on the very principles of academic freedom and open discourse.

The chilling message sent by this incident was clear: conformity is safe, dissent is dangerous. Academic institutions are supposed to be places where ideas can be tested, where challenging existing paradigms is not only welcomed but encouraged as a means of collective growth. Yet Evergreen State College's response to Weinstein's objection revealed a profound shift away from these foundational ideals. The environment had become one where ideological conformity was not only expected but enforced, and where the cost of challenging the status quo could be one's career, reputation, or even personal safety.

The broader implications of Weinstein's experience are profound and troubling. Academia, which should serve as the ultimate arena for the free exchange of ideas, has increasingly become a place where ideological conformity is demanded, and any deviation is met with swift and severe punishment. This phenomenon does not just affect individual scholars like Weinstein, it sends ripples throughout the entire academic community, discouraging others, students, educators, researchers, from exploring complex or controversial topics out of fear of being vilified, ostracized, or worse. The very essence of higher education is to pursue truth, to test ideas through rigorous debate, to confront one's own biases, and to learn through exposure to differing perspectives. When that process is short-circuited by the pressures of cancel culture, we lose out on opportunities for growth, both at an individual and societal level.

The Weinstein controversy also serves as a cautionary tale about the dangers of allowing emotional reactivity to override reasoned debate. Instead of engaging with Weinstein's well-intentioned critique, considering his points and potentially finding a more unifying way to achieve inclusiveness, many of his detractors resorted to tactics of intimidation, ostracization, and character assassination. Such tactics run counter to the foundational values of academic institutions, which are environments of thoughtful engagement, where disagreements are opportunities for learning rather than grounds for punishment. This kind of intellectual bullying creates a monolithic culture, one where only certain viewpoints are permitted, and anything outside the accepted norm is treated as a threat. Such an environment stifles creativity, curiosity, and genuine progress, replacing the vibrant diversity of thought with a bland, one-dimensional echo chamber.

Generation Z, often praised for its commitment to social justice and equality, has been at the forefront of these cultural shifts, but there are challenges within that well-intentioned mission. There is an increasing tendency among some in this generation to label any viewpoint that causes discomfort or challenges their beliefs as inherently offensive or harmful. This fragility and lack of resilience have permeated beyond their own cohort, shaping broader societal norms and contributing to a decline in respect for robust discourse and debate. The so-called "snowflake" mentality, a mindset that rejects resilience and strength in favor of immediate emotional validation, has infiltrated even the highest institutions of learning, places that were once dedicated to cultivating intellectual rigor and strength of character.

When even well-intentioned disagreements are met with aggression, accusations, and a refusal to engage, it sends a simple yet damaging message: the cost of speaking up is too high. This dynamic does not just silence individual voices like Weinstein's, it erodes the very fabric of academic inquiry. Academic freedom cannot exist without the ability to engage in hard conversations, to challenge the status quo, and to explore uncomfortable truths. Without these elements, education becomes little more than indoctrination. To truly advance as a society, we must protect the spaces where tough conversations can happen, where ideas can be tested, challenged, and refined. Otherwise, we risk turning our academic institutions into echo chambers, devoid of the vibrant debate and intellectual diversity that are crucial for both personal and societal growth.

Reversing these troubling trends will require a collective recalibration of our values, a movement away from fragility and entitlement and towards resilience, accountability, and open discourse. Strong leadership within academic institutions is essential to uphold the values of free thought and debate, to resist the pressure to conform at the expense of intellectual diversity. A renewed commitment to personal responsibility, both in controversial ideas and in how we treat those who voice them, is necessary to create environments where learning and growth are prioritized over comfort and conformity. By fostering an atmosphere that rewards intellectual bravery, encourages respectful debate, and promotes resilience, we can restore the integrity of our academic institutions and cultivate a generation of thinkers who are not only capable of tackling the complex challenges of our time but are also unafraid to speak truth, even when it is uncomfortable.

CASE STUDY 3: J.K. ROWLING

J. K. Rowling, the celebrated author of the Harry Potter series, faced significant backlash after expressing her views on gender identity — opinions that some interpreted as transphobic. Despite her longstanding support for LGBTQ+ causes, Rowling's comments on the complexities of gender sparked intense controversy. Many fans who once admired her called for boycotts of her work, and online critics launched campaigns aimed at undermining both her character and her literary legacy. Social media platforms became battlegrounds where her words were dissected, criticized, and amplified by those eager to denounce her. The backlash was swift, with many people reducing her entire identity and contributions to a few controversial statements, disregarding her history of philanthropy.

Rowling's experience is a potent example of how modern cancel culture often disregards the full context of an individual's beliefs or actions, favoring instead a swift and unforgiving condemnation. The reaction to her comments reveals a troubling trend, where even a slight deviation from the accepted narrative can lead to a vicious cycle of public shaming, ostracism, and character assassination. This phenomenon sends a chilling message: even those with a track record of supporting progressive causes can find themselves isolated if their views do not align perfectly with the prevailing ideology. In such an environment, people are incentivized to self-censor rather than engage in meaningful dialogue, fearing that even the slightest misstep could lead to irreparable damage to their reputation and career.

The situation with Rowling is not an isolated incident; it reflects a broader societal issue where the expectation is complete ideological conformity, leaving no space for nuanced discussions. The backlash she faced overlooks the complexity of the issue she sought to discuss, as well as her previous contributions to the LGBTQ+ community. Rowling has long used her influence to advocate for marginalized groups, donating substantial amounts to charities and using her platform to promote equality. However, this context was almost entirely disregarded in the face of her comments on gender, with critics choosing to focus on what they perceived as transphobia, rather than considering her broader history of advocacy.

This phenomenon highlights a dangerous erosion of intellectual freedom. Historically, progress has always relied on the ability to debate, question, and explore complex issues. The pursuit of truth and understanding is tied to our capacity to consider differing perspectives, to challenge established norms, and to question what we think we know. When influential voices are silenced through relentless attacks, society loses the opportunity for nuanced discussions that might foster a deeper understanding of controversial topics. Silencing figures like Rowling, rather than engaging with their perspectives, means losing out on an opportunity for all sides to learn, grow, and potentially find common ground.

The issue here is not simply about J. K. Rowling or her views on gender; it is emblematic of a broader cultural shift where disagreement is conflated with hostility and where ideological conformity is demanded without room for complexity or individuality. Such an atmosphere stifles genuine progress, creating a chilling effect that discourages open dialogue. It leaves little room for growth, reconciliation, or the evolution of ideas. When those with differing perspectives are systematically vilified, it does nothing to advance understanding; instead, it fosters an echo chamber where only certain opinions are permitted, ultimately weakening the very causes it aims to protect. True progress, especially on complex issues like gender identity, can only occur through engagement and dialogue, not through suppression and ostracism.

Rowling's case serves as a cautionary tale about the perils of unchecked cancel culture. It reveals how even well-intentioned individuals who have a history of progressive advocacy can be turned into pariahs for expressing opinions that challenge or complicate the status quo. This type of environment destroys the values of a society that claims to embrace diversity and freedom of thought. In a society that truly values diversity, it is vital to remember that true diversity includes a range of thoughts, beliefs, and opinions. Diversity is not just about identity; it is also about the ideas and perspectives that individuals bring to the table. Without the willingness to listen, to understand, and to respectfully disagree, we risk creating a cultural landscape where fear reigns and genuine progress is stifled.

The implications are far-reaching, not only for public figures like Rowling but for all individuals who wish to take part in important cultural conversations. If even the most prominent voices can be silenced or smeared for expressing nuanced or unpopular views, what hope is there for those without a platform or influence? The culture of immediate outrage, devoid of deeper understanding, discourages people from speaking up, from questioning, and from contributing to the societal discourse. This is not the environment that fosters progress; it is one that breeds conformity and discourages growth.

To move forward, society must cultivate an atmosphere that encourages open conversation, where people feel safe to express their thoughts without the fear of being exiled. It is crucial to distinguish between harmful rhetoric that truly undermines the rights and dignity of others and thoughtful critique that invites reflection, even if it challenges widely accepted beliefs. Only by embracing complexity, by being willing to listen and understand, and by extending grace to those who may make mistakes, can we create a culture that truly embodies progress and empathy.

The case of J. K. Rowling should serve as a reminder that disagreement is not equivalent to hate, and questioning does not equate to harm. It is a call for a recalibration of our cultural values, one that places resilience, understanding, and genuine dialogue above immediate emotional reactivity. By embracing these principles, we can build a society that values diversity not only in identity but in ideas, creating a more inclusive space for everyone to take part in meaningful discussions that drive actual change.

PROTESTS AT UNIVERSITIES: STIFLING INTELLECTUAL DIVERSITY

University campuses are increasingly becoming echo chambers because of the effects of cancel culture, which has a suppressive influence on intellectual diversity and open debate. Historically, universities were celebrated as sanctuaries of free speech, places where young minds were encouraged to challenge prevailing ideas, confront uncomfortable truths, and engage with a wide spectrum of viewpoints. The purpose of higher education was not merely to impart knowledge but to foster the ability to think critically, to question assumptions, and to engage with others whose experiences and beliefs differed from one's own. Yet, in recent times, many campuses have moved away from these ideals, suppressing dissent and silencing differing thoughts, often driven by the actions of Gen Z students who see certain perspectives as inherently harmful or offensive.

Universities, which were once bastions of rigorous debate and intellectual exploration, are now transforming into laboratories of conformity, where disagreement is frequently equated with moral failing. This shift in campus culture undermines the fundamental purpose of education, which is to expose students to challenging ideas, test their beliefs, and strengthen their ability to engage thoughtfully and respectfully with others. Instead of being environments where diversity of thought is celebrated, universities have cultivated a culture that prioritizes comfort over intellectual growth. The prevailing sentiment has become one where avoiding discomfort is more important than seeking truth, leading to a decline in the quality of discourse and a reluctance to confront ideas that may provoke or challenge.

This change in academic culture leaves students ill-prepared for the realities of the world beyond the university setting — a world that does not come with trigger warnings or safe spaces. Outside the protective bubble of the university, individuals must navigate a complex and often challenging landscape filled with differing opinions, conflicts, and the need for resilience. The real world requires individuals to cope with discomfort, to handle criticism, and to engage with those who see the world in different ways. However, by shielding students from controversial or uncomfortable viewpoints, universities are failing to prepare them for these realities. Instead of nurturing resilience, these institutions are fostering fragility, encouraging students to view opposing viewpoints as threats to their emotional wellbeing rather than as opportunities for growth and understanding.

The implications of this shift are significant. The process of learning involves discomfort. Growth occurs when individuals are pushed beyond their current understanding, when they are exposed to ideas that challenge their worldview, and when they are forced to wrestle with complex, sometimes unsettling questions. In the absence of this process, education becomes shallow and incomplete. Students may graduate with degrees, but they lack the critical thinking skills, and the emotional maturity needed to thrive in an environment where not everyone shares their values or perspectives. Instead of cultivating intellectual bravery, universities are inadvertently teaching students that the best way to handle discomfort is to avoid it altogether, to silence it, or to label it as dangerous.

The reduction of universities to echo chambers does not just harm the students themselves; it also has broader consequences for society. When the next generation of leaders, innovators, and thinkers is trained in an environment that suppresses dissent and equates disagreement with harm, we risk creating a culture that is ill-equipped to handle complex social issues. The ability to navigate and mediate between differing viewpoints is crucial for any functioning society. It is through the clash of ideas that better solutions are often found that progress is made, and that individuals learn to see the world from perspectives other than their own.

By fostering a culture where intellectual conformity is expected and enforced, universities also risk alienating those who do not adhere to the dominant ideology. Students and faculty members who hold unpopular or nonmainstream views are often marginalized; their voices drowned out by the demand for consensus. This not only diminishes the diversity of thought on campus but also discourages individuals from speaking up, sharing their ideas, or engaging in meaningful debate. The message is clear: to be accepted, one must conform. These dynamics stifle creativity, discourages innovation, and ultimately undermines the pursuit of knowledge, which should be the core mission of any educational institution.

The role of the university should be to equip students with the tools they need to navigate a world filled with complexity and uncertainty. This includes the ability to engage with ideas they may find uncomfortable, to debate respectfully, and to change their minds when confronted with compelling evidence. It is about learning how to disagree without dehumanizing the other side, about understanding that one's own perspective is not the only valid perspective, and about recognizing that truth is often found through the collision of differing ideas. When universities cannot provide this kind of education, they fail in their responsibility to their students and to society at large.

To reverse these troubling trends, universities must recommit to the values of intellectual diversity and open discourse. This means creating environments where all ideas, even those that are controversial or unpopular, can be expressed and examined. It means encouraging students to engage with viewpoints that differ from their own, not to shut them down. It requires leadership that will stand up for the principles of free speech and to resist the pressures of conformity that threaten to undermine the educational mission. Only by doing so can universities fulfill their role as places where young people are not only educated but also challenged, where they learn not what to think, but how to think.

Ultimately, the goal of higher education should be to prepare students for a complex world, one where they will encounter a diverse range of people, ideas, and challenges. This preparation cannot happen in an environment that prioritizes emotional comfort over intellectual rigor, or that encourages students to equate disagreement with personal harm. By fostering resilience, encouraging open dialogue, and creating space for genuine intellectual exploration, universities can once again become the vibrant centers of learning and growth they were always meant to be. It is only in such environments that true progress can occur, where students can leave not just with knowledge, but with the strength and skills needed to contribute meaningfully to society.

PROTESTS LEADING TO SPEAKER DISINVITATIONS

Disinvitations are a direct attack on free speech and academic exchange. The rise in protests aimed at canceling events and disinviting speakers whose perspectives do not align with the prevailing orthodoxy has created an atmosphere of fear and intellectual submission. Universities, which are the cornerstone of free inquiry and a marketplace of ideas, have increasingly become environments where only certain perspectives may be heard. The pressure to conform to a singular narrative often leads to decisions that undermine the foundational principles of education.

Take, for instance, the 2017 incident at Middlebury College, where controversial author Charles Murray was invited to speak. Murray, whose work and ideas have been subjects of significant debate, was invited hoping to foster a rigorous exchange of viewpoints. However, instead of allowing his ideas to be heard and debated openly, the event devolved into chaos. The protests were not peaceful acts of disagreement but escalated into aggressive disruption, with shouting and physical intimidation that prevented Murray from presenting his ideas. The situation culminated in him being physically attacked and the event prematurely ended, showcasing how far some individuals will go to silence a perspective they found objectionable.

This incident at Middlebury was far from an isolated event. Conservative commentator Ann Coulter has also faced multiple disinvitations from universities across the United States. Student activists have repeatedly deemed her views unfit for academic spaces, resulting in the cancellation of her planned talks. The argument made by these activists is often that certain ideas are too dangerous or offensive to be even considered, but this stance is fundamentally at odds with the core mission of higher education. The purpose of universities is not to protect students from discomfort but to expose them to a wide range of ideas, including those that challenge their existing beliefs. Intellectual growth occurs when we engage with thoughts that make us uncomfortable, that force us to reconsider our positions, and that ultimately make our understanding of the world more nuanced and complete.

The notion that certain ideas are so dangerous that they should not even be presented or debated is antithetical to the purpose of higher education. Universities should be arenas of vigorous debate, where controversial viewpoints are examined and challenged through reasoned argumentation, not silenced through protest and disinvitation. When students are sheltered from challenges, they miss out on the opportunity to develop the critical thinking skills that are essential for navigating a complex and diverse world. Instead of learning how to engage respectfully with opposing views, they learn to shut down conversations they dislike.

The Foundation for Individual Rights in Education, commonly known as FIRE, has documented an alarming increase in disinvitations and speech restrictions on college campuses. According to FIRE, this trend shows a broader cultural shift in which universities, rather than standing as the last line of defense for free expression, are increasingly capitulating to activist pressures. University administrations, fearing backlash and controversy, often choose to cancel events or disinvite speakers rather than uphold the principles of academic freedom and open dialogue. This response not only undermines the integrity of the institutions themselves but also sends a troubling message to students: that it is acceptable to silence those with whom you disagree, rather than confronting their arguments through debate.

The consequences of this trend are far-reaching. When universities prioritize avoiding controversy over fostering open dialogue, they condition a generation of students to reject debate in favor of silencing opposition. Students learn that the response to ideas they find objectionable is not to engage or refute them, but to prevent them from being heard. This mentality breeds intellectual fragility, as students are shielded from the robust debate that is essential for developing resilience, open-mindedness, and the capacity for critical analysis. It also undermines one of the fundamental values of a democratic society — the ability to engage in dialogue across differences and to coexist with people whose views may differ vastly from one's own.

The suppression of speakers like Charles Murray and Ann Coulter is emblematic of a growing intolerance for ideological diversity within academic spaces. When only certain viewpoints are allowed, universities become echo chambers, reinforcing a narrow set of ideas rather than encouraging a diversity of thought. This kind of intellectual homogeneity is dangerous because it stifles innovation, creativity, and progress. New ideas and solutions are born out of the collision of differing perspectives, out of the willingness to consider alternatives, and out of the courage to challenge prevailing wisdom. When this process is curtailed, the entire purpose of higher education—to expand knowledge, to explore complexities, and to cultivate informed citizens—is compromised.

The impact is not limited to the speakers themselves, who are often portrayed as villains in these scenarios, but also extends to the students who are denied the opportunity to hear diverse perspectives. When students are not exposed to a range of viewpoints, they are ill-prepared for the complexities of the real world, where not everyone will share their opinions and where they will need to engage constructively with people who think differently. Shielding students from controversial ideas may create a temporary sense of comfort, but it ultimately does them a disservice by failing to equip them with the tools they need to navigate a world full of diverse beliefs and values.

If we are to uphold the mission of higher education, universities must recommit to being spaces of open inquiry, where ideas are tested, debated, and refined through the process of critical engagement. This does not mean that all viewpoints are equally valid or that harmful rhetoric should be given a platform without challenge. Rather, it means that the response to ideas we disagree with should be to confront them with better arguments, not to shut them down. It means recognizing that the ability to engage with difficult and sometimes uncomfortable ideas is a crucial part of the educational experience and one that is essential for personal and intellectual growth.

The path forward requires strong leadership from university administrations, a renewed commitment to the principles of academic freedom, and a recognition that true learning comes from confronting complexity, not avoiding it. Universities should encourage students to listen, to question, and to engage—not to fear ideas that challenge them. By fostering an environment where intellectual diversity is celebrated and debate is encouraged, universities can fulfill their role as incubators of knowledge, innovation, and informed citizenship. Only then can we hope to prepare the next generation to be thoughtful, resilient, and capable of contributing meaningfully to the world.

THE DANGERS OF CENSORSHIP AND IDEOLOGICAL CONFORMITY

This dangerous trend does more than just undermine free speech; it erodes the core of what it truly means to receive an education. Intellectual diversity is not a luxury in academia; it is an absolute necessity. Exposure to diverse perspectives, especially those that challenge our own, is crucial for developing critical thinking skills. The heart of education lies in confronting differing viewpoints, wrestling with complex ideas, and learning to articulate well-reasoned arguments in response. Without the ability to confront and grapple with difficult or even offensive ideas, students are left ill-prepared for the nuanced challenges of life beyond the university setting. By sheltering students from controversial speakers or opinions, universities hinder the development of independent thought, resilience, and maturity—qualities that are essential not only for academic success but for navigating the complexities of the world.

The ideological conformity taking root on many campuses today is entirely antithetical to the foundation of progress itself. Social progress has never been about maintaining comfort or avoiding conflict. It has always depended on the challenge of prevailing norms and the open discussion of ideas, even those that are unpopular or offensive. When universities suppress this vital discourse in favor of promoting ideological homogeneity, they do not eliminate the ideas that are deemed problematic; instead, they merely drive them underground. This does not only fail to eradicate these ideas but fosters resentment and deepens social division. When people feel that their views are being systematically silenced or ignored, the result is often a sense of alienation that makes meaningful dialogue and reconciliation even more difficult. Refusing to engage with controversial ideas does not eliminate them, it simply dismisses their prevalence and pushes them into spaces where they cannot be challenged or scrutinized.

In an age where universities should nurture intellectual bravery, they are instead breeding cowardice by wrapping students in a cocoon of agreeable opinions that leave them fundamentally unprepared for a pluralistic society. The goal of education should be to equip students with the tools to navigate and understand a complex, diverse world where people hold different beliefs, values, and experiences. By shielding students from the discomfort of opposing viewpoints, universities are doing them a disservice. They are cultivating environments where disagreement is harmful rather than an opportunity for growth, and where the goal becomes emotional protection rather than intellectual engagement. When education shifts from fostering understanding and resilience to merely protecting feelings, the very essence of learning is compromised.

The university experience should be challenging. It should involve grappling with difficult texts, engaging with people whose worldviews differ vastly from one's own, and encountering new and sometimes uncomfortable ideas. This process helps students develop resilience, empathy, and the ability to think critically. However, when universities prioritize comfort over challenge, they lose the rigor that makes education meaningful. Instead of fostering debate, encouraging students to question their assumptions, and providing a space where they can grow through intellectual struggle, universities risk becoming factories of ideological uniformity — places where only certain viewpoints are allowed, and where the richness of diverse perspectives is lost.

The consequences of this shift are far-reaching. When students are not exposed to a variety of perspectives, when they are not encouraged to debate and defend their ideas, they are less likely to develop the skills needed to think independently. Independent thought is not something that happens automatically; it must be cultivated through exposure to diverse, sometimes conflicting information, and through the process of questioning and defending one's own beliefs. A campus that values intellectual conformity over diversity of thought fails to provide the kind of education that prepares students for life beyond its walls. In the real world, people are confronted with situations that require them to navigate disagreement, to find common ground, and to respect those with whom they may disagree. Without the opportunity to practice these skills in a university setting, students are left at a disadvantage.

The suppression of controversial ideas creates a false sense of consensus. It gives the illusion that everyone agrees on certain fundamental issues, when many perspectives are simply being silenced. This false consensus does not lead to true understanding or unity. Instead, it creates an environment where difficult topics are avoided, where dissenting voices are marginalized, and where actual progress is stifled. True social progress requires that we engage with all ideas, even those we find uncomfortable or offensive. It requires that we debate, to argue, and to listen, even when the conversation is difficult.

The risk is that universities will lose their status as places of growth and intellectual challenge. Instead of being centers of rigorous academic pursuit, they become places where students are taught what to think, rather than how to think. The danger is not just that students are missing out on important aspects of their education, but that they are being conditioned to view disagreement as something to be feared rather than embraced. They are taught that the proper response to ideas they dislike is to silence those ideas, rather than confront them and provide a stronger argument. This does not lead to powerful individuals. It leads to a generation that cannot engage constructively with those who think differently, and that lacks the tools to navigate the complex, diverse world that awaits them beyond the university.

If universities are to fulfill their mission, they must recommit to fostering environments where intellectual diversity is valued and where debate is encouraged. They must teach students it is not only acceptable to encounter ideas that challenge their beliefs, but that it is essential for their growth. This means standing firm against the pressures to conform, refusing to capitulate to those who would rather see certain ideas silenced than debated. It means encouraging students to take intellectual risks, to be uncomfortable, and to understand that growth often comes through struggle.

By promoting these values, universities can help ensure that they remain places where true learning occurs, where students are not only educated but transformed. Education should be a journey that leaves students better equipped to handle the complexities of life, not more fragile in the face of adversity. It should prepare them to engage with the world as it is, not as they wish it to be. Only by fostering environments of true intellectual diversity and open debate can universities hope to prepare their students for the challenges that lie ahead, ensuring that they leave not only with knowledge but with the resilience and understanding needed to contribute meaningfully to society.

THE CULTURAL SHIFT: FROM LIBERALISM TO THOUGHT POLICING

Liberalism, in theory, has long stood as a defender of free speech and intellectual exploration, a philosophy that ostensibly promoted the value of open discourse and the exchange of diverse perspectives. Traditionally, it embraced the fundamental notion that societal progress emerges from the robust clash of differing viewpoints, where even the most unpopular or controversial ideas are given a platform to be heard. According to the liberal tradition, dissent and diversity of thought are critical for a healthy democracy. Historically, this ethos helped to foster innovation, challenging injustices, and driving societal growth by permitting an array of ideas to be openly debated, tested, and refined.

However, the current state of liberalism has shifted dramatically from its foundational principles, and the rise of cancel culture signals a disturbing and clear departure from these ideals. Liberalism today is increasingly being used not to protect the right to express unpopular views, but as a mechanism to enforce ideological conformity. Rather than championing the free exchange of ideas, it has, frequently, been weaponized to suppress and silence voices that do not align with the dominant ideological narrative. Instead of fostering open debate and healthy dissent, contemporary liberal practices often create an environment where challenging the accepted perspective is deemed unacceptable, and individuals are ostracized for expressing nonconforming views.

The freedom to explore and express conflicting viewpoints, which was once a cornerstone of liberal thought, has been constrained by the expectation that only certain narratives are permissible. This shift has effectively transformed what should have been a platform for dialogue into a system that polices thought and punishes those who dare to deviate from prevailing ideological norms. Rather than encouraging individuals to engage with ideas they disagree with—an essential component of both personal and intellectual growth—this alternative approach is more concerned with shutting down conversations altogether. The growing insistence on conformity has left a chilling effect on free speech, and the genuine diversity of intellectual thought is not only discouraged but often actively suppressed.

This narrowing of permissible viewpoints is clear across academic institutions, social media platforms, and public discourse. Universities, once celebrated as centers of free inquiry and spaces where ideas of all sorts could be freely debated, are increasingly becoming places where only one ideology is accepted. The refusal to allow controversial speakers or to entertain challenging ideas on campuses is symptomatic of a broader problem. Rather than being a place where students learn to grapple with different perspectives and sharpen their thinking, universities have become environments where young minds are shielded from discomfort and dissent. This intellectual sheltering cannot prepare students for the complexities of the real world, where ideas are diverse, disagreements are inevitable and navigating them requires resilience and open-mindedness.

The consequences of this intellectual conformity extend far beyond college campuses. In society at large, there is a growing trend toward intolerance for any viewpoint that deviates from the accepted mainstream narrative. Instead of engaging with opposing perspectives, individuals are encouraged to vilify, dismiss, or outright ignore them. The result is a population that is increasingly incapable of nuanced thinking, where individuals lack the skills or the willingness to engage constructively with those who hold different beliefs. This not only fosters an echo chamber effect but also creates deeper societal divisions, as individuals retreat further into their ideological silos, unwilling or unable to engage with those outside of their belief systems.

Moreover, this shift toward ideological conformity is fundamentally antithetical to the very idea of progress. Social progress, historically, has always been achieved through the challenge of prevailing norms and the open discussion of new, sometimes controversial, ideas. Whether it was the fight for civil rights, the push for women's suffrage, or the advocacy for freedom of expression, progress has relied on the ability of individuals to question the status quo and to present alternative viewpoints. Suppressing this discourse in favor of maintaining ideological homogeneity does not eliminate the ideas deemed problematic; it merely drives them underground, where they may fester, unchallenged and unresolved. Refusing to engage with controversial ideas does not make them disappear; it simply ignores their existence and dismisses their prevalence.

By pushing certain ideas out of the public discourse entirely, society loses the ability to effectively counter them with better arguments and sound reasoning. It is not enough to silence an idea; true progress requires that bad ideas be exposed to scrutiny, debated, and ultimately rejected based on their lack of merit. When society refuses to allow this process to occur, it creates an illusion of consensus, one that is shallow and fragile. Instead of genuinely addressing the root causes of societal issues, this approach relies on coercion and exclusion to maintain order, which ultimately leads to resentment, division, and the entrenchment of those very ideas it seeks to suppress.

In an age where universities and public institutions should be nurturing intellectual bravery, they are instead cultivating an atmosphere of intellectual cowardice. Students are increasingly being wrapped in a cocoon of agreeable opinions that leave them fundamentally unprepared for the pluralistic society they will encounter upon graduation. A healthy, functioning democracy depends on citizens who can engage with a wide range of viewpoints, of understanding perspectives different from their own, and of engaging in productive debate. When the goal of education shifts from fostering understanding and resilience to merely protecting feelings, the essence of learning is compromised, and the ability to engage in meaningful societal contributions is severely diminished.

Universities are at risk of losing their status as places of growth, inquiry, and intellectual challenge. Instead of being centers of rigorous academic pursuit, they are transforming into institutions where students are taught what to think rather than how to think. The result is not an educated populace capable of critical analysis and reasoned debate, but rather a generation conditioned to fear disagreement and to avoid intellectual challenges. Such an environment stifles creativity, limits innovation, and ultimately weakens the very fabric of society by discouraging the diversity of thought that is necessary for true progress.

If society is to advance, it must recommit to the values that have historically underpinned progress: open discourse, freedom of thought, and the willingness to engage with those who see the world differently. This means creating environments where ideas, even those that are controversial or offensive, can be presented, debated, and examined. It means encouraging individuals to confront and engage with ideas that make them uncomfortable, not to shut them down or silence them. It requires strong leadership from academic institutions, media platforms, and public figures to resist the growing pressure to conform and to instead champion the principles of intellectual freedom and open dialogue.

Only by fostering environments where genuine intellectual diversity is valued and debate is encouraged can society hope to address the complex challenges that lie ahead. The trend of promoting ideological conformity under the guise of liberal values does more to harm society than to help it, as it ultimately stifles the critical conversations that are essential for growth and progress. By embracing open debate, by protecting the right to dissent, and by encouraging individuals to think for themselves, society can foster an environment where true progress is not only possible but inevitable.

THE WEAPONIZATION OF LIBERALISM

Today's version of liberalism, often closely linked with identity politics, has evolved into something that demands rigid adherence to specific social narratives. What was once a framework for defending free expression, promoting intellectual diversity, and ensuring individual rights has now, many times, transformed into an ideology that requires conformity and submission to a narrow set of beliefs. This shift is evident in the rise of identity politics, where issues of race, gender, and sexuality have taken center stage, often at the expense of constructive dialogue or including diverse opinions. While these topics are undeniably important and deserving of discussion, the current discourse frequently lacks any nuance, leaving little to no room for meaningful debate or differing perspectives.

In "The Coddling of the American Mind," social psychologist Jonathan Haidt discusses this shift in great detail, highlighting how younger generations are increasingly encouraged to see the world in stark, binary terms. Issues are presented as simple battles between good and evil, heroes and villains, where one's stance determines their moral worth. In this framework, opposing views are not just considered misguided; they are demonized as morally reprehensible, unworthy of engagement, and often deserving of punishment. This shift toward moral absolutism has redefined liberal values, turning what should be instruments of openminded inquiry into tools of ideological enforcement. No longer are people encouraged to wrestle with complex issues, to question, or to engage with perspectives different from their own. Instead, they are instructed to accept prescribed answers without question, lest they be labeled as ignorant, hateful, or even dangerous.

This transformation has had a particularly damaging impact on Generation Z, shaping their collective mindset in ways that are increasingly troubling. Gen Z, growing up in an environment where liberalism is synonymous with conformity, is being conditioned to fear the consequences of deviating from the accepted narrative. The pressure to conform is immense, and the repercussions for stepping out of line are swift and unforgiving. As a result, many members of Gen Z are less likely to engage in the independent, critical thinking that is necessary for both personal growth and societal progress. They learn that their value as individuals is contingent on their adherence to the "correct" set of beliefs and that those who question or challenge the mainstream narrative should be ostracized or punished.

Consider, for example, recent events at Stanford University, where a federal judge invited to speak on campus was shouted down by student activists who disagreed with his legal rulings. Rather than allowing the judge to present his views and then challenging him through reasoned debate, the students prevented him from speaking at all. Worse still, a member of the university's administration publicly supported the students' actions, framing the judge's perspective as inherently harmful and undeserving of an audience. This incident illustrates the environment in which Generation Z is being educated—one in which dissent is not tolerated and where opposing perspectives are not seen as opportunities for learning but as threats to be eradicated. The result is a generation that is increasingly fragile, unaccustomed to engaging with challenging ideas, and prone to shutting down anything that does not align with their worldview.

Another stark example is the recent backlash against bestselling author J. K. Rowling, who expressed her views on gender identity—a topic she felt deserved thoughtful, nuanced discussion. Despite her long history of supporting LGBTQ+ rights, Rowling was met with intense hostility, and efforts were made to cancel her entirely, with calls for boycotting her books and attacks on her character. For members of Gen Z, many of whom are deeply immersed in identity politics, this type of reaction becomes the norm—a learned behavior that reinforces the notion that anyone who steps out of line, regardless of their intent or history of good deeds, should be vilified. This leads to an environment where nuanced debate is not only discouraged but actively prevented, and the focus becomes punishment rather than understanding.

The impact of these dynamics on Generation Z is particularly concerning because this is a cohort that has grown up surrounded by these ideologies. In classrooms and on social media platforms, they are exposed to a narrow set of acceptable ideas, and deviation is treated as a moral failing. Critical thinking, which is the bedrock of intellectual growth, is being replaced by an emphasis on ideological purity. This has created a mindset where members of Gen Z are not only afraid to express dissenting opinions but are often unwilling to even entertain them. They are more inclined to see opposing viewpoints as personal attacks rather than as opportunities for discussion, and they have been conditioned to seek validation in echo chambers where everyone agrees rather than in environments where ideas are challenged and debated.

The rise of identity politics has further compounded this problem. While identity politics initially sought to bring attention to the struggles of marginalized groups, it has since evolved into a divisive force that categorizes individuals based on immutable traits, such as race, gender, or sexual orientation, and then assigns moral value based on these traits. This framework teaches Gen Z that their identity is paramount, and that the identity of others determines the legitimacy of their viewpoints. As a result, discussions are no longer about the merits of an idea but about who is expressing it. This leads to a climate where intellectual diversity is stifled, and engaging with someone from a different background or with a different perspective is seen as unnecessary or even dangerous.

The consequences of this are evident in the workplace, where members of Gen Z are entering in large numbers.

Employers increasingly report that young employees are ill-equipped to handle disagreement or criticism. They expect workplaces to function like the universities they attend, places where dissent is limited, and ideological conformity is the norm. This mindset is problematic because it runs counter to the realities of the professional world, where diverse perspectives are crucial for innovation and where disagreements are a natural part of problem-solving. Instead of developing resilience, the ability to navigate complex social dynamics, and the capacity to work with people who hold different views, many members of Gen Z are entering the workforce with an expectation that their beliefs should not be challenged and that those who disagree with them should be silenced.

Social media, a pervasive force in the lives of Gen Z, has amplified these problems. Platforms like Twitter and TikTok, which reward users for aligning with popular opinions and punishing those who express dissenting views, have further entrenched the mindset of ideological conformity. On these platforms, the consequences of stepping outside of the accepted narrative can be swift and brutal, often involving public shaming and the threat of being "canceled." This has taught an entire generation to prioritize the approval of the crowd over independent thought, and to view social validation as more important than truth or integrity. The echo chamber effect, where algorithms serve content that reinforces existing beliefs, has only deepened this divide, leaving little opportunity for young people to encounter or engage with viewpoints that differ from their own.

The consequences of these trends cannot be overstated. Liberalism, in its current form, no longer defends the individual's right to think freely or to speak without fear of reprisal. Instead, it has become a tool for enforcing conformity, and it is Generation Z who is most affected by this transformation. This generation, raised in an environment where intellectual diversity is dangerous and where dissent is punished rather than explored, is at risk of being the least resilient, the least openminded, and the least capable of navigating the complexities of a pluralistic society. They are not taught to engage with challenging ideas but to fear them, not to debate their opponents but to silence them, and not to grow through discomfort but to avoid it at all costs.

If we are to correct this trajectory, we must return to the foundational principles that made liberalism a force for progress. We must foster environments—in schools, universities, workplaces, and online—where intellectual diversity is celebrated, where debate is encouraged, and where disagreement is seen as an opportunity for growth rather than a threat. Generation Z must be taught that the world is complex, that people will disagree, and that the ability to engage with those who hold different beliefs is not just a skill—

it is a requirement for personal growth and for the health of a democratic society.

The current trajectory of liberalism, entwined with identity politics and growing intolerance for dissent, poses a significant threat to the foundational values of free expression, open dialogue, and genuine diversity of thought. It is time to reclaim the principles that once made liberalism a force for progress — principles that celebrated the freedom to think, to speak, and to challenge. Only by doing so can we hope to foster a Generation Z that is resilient, dynamic, and capable of facing the challenges of the future without fear or conformity, prepared not just to navigate the real world, but to shape it for the better.

ENFORCING CONFORMITY THROUGH SOCIAL PRESSURE

Social media plays an integral role in the enforcement of ideological conformity that we see today. Platforms like Twitter, Instagram, and Facebook have amplified outrage to an unprecedented degree, making it easier than ever to publicly shame individuals who express opinions that deviate from the accepted narrative. The rise of this type of digital mob mentality has resulted in a culture where people are increasingly afraid to share any perspective that might challenge the status quo. Instead of being a place for open debate and the exchange of ideas, social media has turned into a collection of echo chambers where only certain perspectives are allowed to flourish, while dissenting voices are systematically silenced.

The problem with social media platforms is not just the creation of echo chambers but also the deliberate suppression of specific viewpoints through mechanisms that are presented as impartial. Facebook, for instance, has been a notorious example of this bias. It has been reported in mainstream media that during election cycles, Facebook actively censored individuals whose viewpoints did not align with the preferred narrative. Under the guise of combating misinformation, the platform used "factcheckers" to flag and suppress content that ran counter to what was deemed acceptable. These factcheckers were often affiliated with organizations that held clear ideological biases, calling into question their ability to be fair arbiters of truth. As a result, the platform developed a reputation for enforcing a particular political narrative, effectively curtailing the free exchange of ideas and influencing public discourse during critical moments, such as national elections.

Moreover, reports have also highlighted Facebook's biases against themes that do not align with the current social orthodoxy, including its strong bias against Christian content. Multiple instances have been documented where posts with Christian themes or viewpoints were flagged, restricted, or even removed under the vague justification of violating community guidelines. This bias against religious themes that diverge from mainstream secular ideology underscores the platform's active role in dictating which beliefs are acceptable for public consumption. The enforcement of such one-sided content regulation is not merely an issue of platform policy, it represents a direct attack on the intellectual and ideological diversity that is necessary for a healthy, functioning democracy.

Social media platforms have evolved from being tools for communication and connection into instruments of control and conformity. By amplifying outrage and penalizing dissent, they have created an environment of high social pressure where individuals are deterred from expressing their true opinions. Studies in social psychology confirm that environments characterized by high levels of social pressure lead to a suppression of true opinions, as individuals fear the potential social, professional, or even personal consequences of expressing dissenting views. In such an atmosphere, people quickly learn that staying silent or publicly conforming to the majority view is the safer option, even if it means suppressing their genuine beliefs. This fear of social ostracization creates a chilling effect that extends far beyond the digital realm, influencing behavior in workplaces, academic settings, and personal relationships.

This dynamic has resulted in a vicious cycle where groupthink prevails, and intellectual diversity becomes increasingly rare. When individuals are discouraged from speaking their minds, the perception of consensus grows, creating an illusion that everyone agrees with the dominant narrative. This illusion of unanimity only serves to further entrench the prevailing ideology, making it even more dangerous for anyone to step out of line. The suppression of differing viewpoints does not lead to a more informed or united society, it leads to a more fragile one, where dissent is hidden rather than addressed, and the actual complexities of societal issues are ignored in favor of simplistic, one-dimensional narratives.

Take, for instance, how Facebook handled discussions about the COVID19 pandemic. Any content that did not align with the official positions on topics like vaccine efficacy, lockdowns, or treatment methods was frequently flagged, suppressed, or removed entirely. Voices from medical professionals who raised questions about alternative treatments or government mandates were silenced, their content labeled as "misinformation" even though scientific understanding is inherently evolving. This suppression effectively stifled legitimate debate and inquiry, leaving only one narrative available for public consumption. That scientific and social debates should be open to scrutiny and discussion was replaced with a rigid insistence on conformity, enforced by tech giants who took it upon themselves to decide what made up the "truth."

The consequences of such actions are significant, particularly for the younger generation—Generation Z—who have grown up with social media as a central aspect of their lives. This generation is being conditioned to view disagreement as inherently dangerous, something to be silenced rather than discussed. They see people who express unpopular opinions being publicly shamed, losing their jobs, or facing personal attacks. As a result, many members of Gen Z have internalized the belief that safety comes from conformity and that challenging dominant idea is simply not worth the risk. This is particularly concerning given that Gen Z is often portrayed as a progressive and socially conscious generation. Yet, the very platforms that have shaped their worldview discourage them from embracing the true meaning of progress, which is built on the robust exchange of differing ideas.

The echo chamber effect on social media has also contributed to a broader social fragmentation, where individuals are increasingly isolated from those who hold different beliefs. Algorithms designed to maximize engagement prioritize content that aligns with users' existing views, reinforcing their beliefs and shielding them from opposing perspectives. This isolation is dangerous because it fosters intolerance and a lack of empathy. When people are never exposed to ideas that challenge their own, they become less capable of understanding or relating to those who think differently. This kind of intellectual insularity is the breeding ground for the divisiveness and polarization we see in society today.

Facebook's role in perpetuating this fragmentation is evident in its handling of political content during election cycles. Reports have surfaced indicating that Facebook took deliberate actions to suppress conservative viewpoints while allowing content that aligned with its preferred political narrative to spread without scrutiny. This kind of selective censorship has profound implications for the democratic process. It distorts public discourse, giving undue influence to one side of the political spectrum and effectively silencing the other. The result is not a more informed electorate but a manipulated one, where the marketplace of ideas—a foundational principle of democracy—is skewed in favor of those who hold the power to control the flow of information.

The problem extends to other platforms as well. Twitter, under its previous leadership, was notorious for banning users who violated its everchanging and often inconsistently applied rules regarding hate speech and misinformation. High-profile accounts, including those of political figures, were permanently suspended for expressing views that were deemed harmful, while others, who expressed similarly extreme views from an opposing ideological stance, faced no such consequences. This selective enforcement of rules reveals a blatant bias that undermines the credibility of these platforms as fair arbiters of public discourse. Instead of providing a forum for the exchange of ideas, they have become gatekeepers, determining which ideas are allowed to be part of the conversation and which are not.

The suppression of Christian content on Facebook further underscores the ideological bias that permeates these platforms. Posts discussing Christian beliefs, traditional values, or even merely quoting scripture have been flagged as hate speech, restricted, or outright removed. This is ironic given that liberalism once stood for protecting minority voices and the right to freely express one's beliefs. Today, however, it appears that the protection of expression only applies to those who align with a particular secular, progressive ideology. This bias against Christian themes and content sends a clear message that certain beliefs are unwelcome in the public square, and it discourages individuals from expressing their faith openly for fear of reprisal.

These dynamics contribute to a deeply unhealthy social environment, one where fear of social exclusion overrides the pursuit of truth. Platforms that should serve as modern-day public squares have become arenas of ideological enforcement, where only approved narratives may thrive. For Generation Z, the consequences of growing up in this environment are dire. They are inheriting a culture where ideological conformity is virtuous and where the fear of being "canceled" is ever-present. Instead of being encouraged to think critically, to question, and to engage with those who see the world differently, they are being taught that the safest course of action is to stay silent, to nod in agreement, and to avoid any conversation that might be deemed controversial.

The long-term implications of this mindset are profound. A generation that is afraid to speak freely is a generation that will struggle to innovate, to lead, and to bring about meaningful change. True progress requires courage to challenge prevailing norms, to question authority, and to propose new ideas, even when they are unpopular. The current trajectory of social media, with its biases, its echo chambers, and its penchant for punishing dissent, is creating a generation that lacks this courage. If we are to move forward as a society, we must push back against this culture of enforced conformity. We must demand that social media platforms live up to their promise of being spaces for free expression and open debate. And we must teach the next generation that the answer to bad ideas is not to silence them but to confront them with better ones.

The role of social media in fostering this environment of ideological conformity and intellectual fragility cannot be ignored. Platforms like Facebook, Twitter, and Instagram have moved far beyond their original purposes of connection and community. They have become powerful tools of social control, dictating which ideas are acceptable and which are not. For the sake of free speech, intellectual diversity, and the future of a healthy society, it is imperative that we reclaim these platforms as spaces for genuine dialogue, where all voices can be heard, and where the value of an idea is determined not by who says it, but by its merits in the marketplace of thought. Only then can we hope to foster a culture that values truth over conformity, debate over silence, and courage over fear.

A CULTURE AT RISK

The rise of wokeness and cancel culture endangers free speech and intellectual diversity. While these movements began with good intentions seeking to address historical injustices and promote inclusivity, they have morphed into tools for policing thought, enforcing conformity, and punishing those who dare to step outside the narrow confines of what is considered socially acceptable. The outcome has been a chilling effect on free speech, where individuals, institutions, and even corporations are forced into silence or compelled to adopt positions that align with the dominant cultural orthodoxy for fear of being targeted, ostracized, or completely erased from public life.

What initially started as a movement to bring about much-needed change has been twisted into a modern-day inquisition, where words are weaponized and genuine curiosity is suffocated by fear. Cancel culture, in its current form, resembles a mob mentality a digital pitchfork that strikes without nuance, leaving no room for understanding, context, or growth. The public discourse has devolved into an environment where disagreement is automatically seen as malicious rather than a natural and necessary component of a healthy society. Disagreement, debate, and the questioning of ideas have driven human progress since the Enlightenment; yet we are now seeing these pillars of civil society crumble in the face of an ideology that is intolerant of dissent.

Those who call for "accountability" under the banner of cancel culture often cannot recognize that accountability is not synonymous with collective punishment or perpetual exile. True accountability involves understanding, reconciliation, and the possibility of redemption. Cancel culture thrives on quick judgment and public shaming, targeting individuals for past mistakes in different contexts. It is as though we have adopted an unforgiving doctrine, one that denies the complexity of human growth and refuses to acknowledge that people are capable of change. This rigidness is not only destructive to individuals but also to society at large, as it deters people from participating in open dialogue or voicing opinions that might be construed as controversial, even if those opinions are held in good faith.

The broader consequence of cancel culture's unchecked growth is the normalization of intellectual cowardice. People, particularly those in influential positions academics, journalists, entertainers, even business leaders are now self-censoring out of fear. The range of permissible thought is shrinking, and with it, the richness of our collective conversation. Ideas are no longer evaluated on their merits but are instead filtered through the lens of ideological purity. This creates a perilous situation where entire topics are deemed off-limits, where entire groups of people feel unheard, and where society loses its capacity for critical thinking. If all we hear are echoes of the same opinions, we risk intellectual stagnation and miss opportunities to solve complex problems that require multiple perspectives.

If cancel culture continues unchecked, the risk is that open debate will be replaced by a culture of fear, where only certain views are permissible, and dissent is swiftly and mercilessly punished. We will find ourselves in a society that superficially celebrates diversity while, in reality, repressing the most important kind of diversity: diversity of thought. It is not hyperbolic to say that this is a direct threat to democracy itself. When people are no longer free to express differing opinions without fear of retribution, the foundation of a free and open society is in jeopardy.

Reversing this trend will require a recommitment to the original core values of liberalism: dialogue, tolerance, and a willingness to engage with differing perspectives. This means protecting the rights of those we disagree with to express their views however unpopular they might be. It means promoting open debate and redemption instead of exclusion. Inclusivity means understanding and accepting different perspectives.

To overcome conformity and stagnation, we must rebuild space for dialogue and tolerance. We need to move past the performative wokeness that has taken center stage, and focus instead on building bridges, fostering empathy, and nurturing a culture that values learning over punishment. Only then can we truly progress as a society not by enforcing rigid conformity, but by celebrating and learning from our differences.

CHAPTER FOUR

MENTAL HEALTH, VICTIMHOOD, AND FRAGILITY

The increasing conversation around mental health, particularly among Gen Z, has undeniably led to heightened awareness of critical issues like anxiety, depression, and trauma. It has illuminated struggles that previous generations often concealed, dragging them from the shadows and placing them under the bright, empathetic spotlight of modern discourse. This shift has led to people being more open about seeking help and discussing mental health.

But beneath the surface of this apparent progress lies a disturbing trend that is eroding the foundation of resilience in our youth. What began as a compassionate movement to destigmatize mental health has, for many, devolved into a culture of fragility and self-imposed victimhood. The language of trauma and anxiety, originally intended to foster understanding and healing, has mutated into a lexicon of excuses. It has become a convenient shield, providing young people with justification for retreating from adversity rather than facing it head-on. The focus on mental health as a defining characteristic has led to a generation comfortable identifying as broken.

This chapter explores how this phenomenon has unfolded. Self-diagnosis through social media platforms has played a pivotal role in cultivating a generation that identifies more readily with its ailments than its strengths. TikTok and Instagram are rife with influencers dispensing pseudo psychological advice, offering mental health diagnoses like anxiety or ADHD without any formal training or understanding of nuance. The result is an entire cohort of young people defining themselves by labels, self-applied and often incorrect, that serve to limit rather than liberate. Instead of seeking solutions, they seek sympathy; instead of engaging in the arduous work of personal growth, they declare their obstacles insurmountable.

The notion of victimhood has become an insidious form of identity. In a society that increasingly rewards public displays of struggle that sees vulnerability not as a step toward strength but as an end, Gen Z has internalized a damaging belief: that their value comes from their suffering. Hardships are no longer moments to overcome, but badges to wear, proof of one's authenticity and depth. Rather than cultivating resilience, many are encouraged to amplify their wounds. They are incentivized to avoid triggers, to cut off anyone or anything that challenges their mental comfort, and to lean into avoidance rather than adaptation. Such an environment stunts the development of crucial life skills, like perseverance and adaptability, which have been the cornerstone of American grit and success for generations.

In this cultural context, adversity is no longer something to be conquered but something to be avoided. And when adversity is avoided, so too are the opportunities for growth and maturity. Challenges which once forged character, resilience, and ultimately, self-respect are now seen as intolerable threats to one's mental health. Gen Z's psyche is now embedded with a culture of fragility due to glorifying safe spaces and constant emotional coddling.

The ramifications of this are profound. The avoidance of personal challenges has not only stunted the emotional growth of individuals but also weakened the collective fabric of our society. When young people are taught to see themselves primarily as victims as fragile beings incapable of weathering life's inevitable storms, they become dependent. They look outward for rescue rather than inward for strength. This dependency erodes not only personal accountability but also the communal values that bind a society together. A culture that celebrates fragility over resilience is one that cannot hope to thrive in the face of global challenges, economic pressures, or even the day-to-day demands of life.

To reverse this trend, we must recalibrate our collective narrative around mental health. We must champion resilience as much as we do empathy. Mental health struggles are real, and seeking help is vital, but these truths should not come at the cost of abandoning the concept of personal strength. We must teach young people that acknowledging a problem is only the first step what comes next is the hard work of overcoming it. Real empowerment lies not in embracing victimhood, but in defying it. We need a cultural shift that celebrates not just vulnerability, but also the courage to rise above it, to confront challenges, and to emerge stronger on the other side.

This is the crux of our challenge: to reclaim the values of accountability, perseverance, and resilience. Gen Z needs to be reminded that character and purpose are built through determination, not a desire for protection.

MENTAL HEALTH AWARENESS VS. MENTAL HEALTH DEPENDENCY

Mental health awareness has indeed become a rallying cry for Gen Z, a generation that prides itself on destigmatizing anxiety, depression, and trauma like no group before them. At face value, this cultural shift is commendable, shining a light on issues that have been shrouded in darkness for too long. But what started as an essential movement for emotional transparency has now taken a troubling turn. Instead of using mental health awareness to build strength, many Gen Z members have weaponized it as an excuse for inaction and fragility.

A critical line has been crossed. Awareness was once crucial for personal growth, but now it's often used as an excuse to avoid life's demands. The pendulum has swung from awareness to dependency, fostering an environment where emotional struggles are allowed to define personal limits rather than overcome them. There is no progress being made now. It is a culture of fragility disguised as enlightenment.

Gen Z often wears mental health challenges as badges of identity, cloaking themselves in diagnostic labels that were never intended to be permanent fixtures of personality. The idea that struggling emotionally justifies disengaging from societal expectations has become normalized. Where previous generations viewed anxiety and adversity as hurdles to clear, Gen Z seems to increasingly view them as immovable roadblocks, validating avoidance rather than conquering fear.

This attitude has real consequences. By insulating themselves from challenges under the guise of "selfcare" or "mental health preservation," many young people are depriving themselves of the resilience that comes only through hardship. True strength is forged in the fires of adversity it is not born from the comfort of avoidance. The historical tenets of resilience, such as perseverance, grit, and the ability to endure and overcome, are being replaced by an ever-growing vocabulary of avoidance and self-protection. This creates a generation ill-equipped to handle even minor setbacks, let alone the significant life challenges that inevitably come.

The issue is further compounded by a society that seems more interested in cushioning the path than encouraging growth. Institutions, educational systems, and even workplaces are increasingly bending over backward to accommodate this fragility, reinforcing the idea that discomfort should be avoided at all costs. It is a dangerous precedent that not only weakens the individual but jeopardizes the resilience of our society. The very fabric of a thriving community depends on the ability of its members to endure, adapt, and grow qualities that are becoming alarmingly rare among today's youth.

To be clear, mental health challenges are real, and the need for support is critical. But support should aim to uplift, empower, and inspire growth not to excuse and enable avoidance. There is a stark difference between being vulnerable and being weak, between seeking help and surrendering to struggle. It is time for a recalibration, a societal pivot back to encouraging young people to face challenges head-on, to recognize that their struggles do not define their limits, but rather present opportunities to surpass them. The true measure of progress is not found in how comfortably we can avoid discomfort, but in how courageously we confront it, grow through it, and emerge stronger on the other side.

This generation has the tools, the technology, and the unprecedented support systems to not only overcome their struggles but to thrive beyond them. What they need is a shift in mindset one that reclaims resilience, embraces adversity, and stops glorifying fragility as a virtue. If we can make that shift, then perhaps the next conversation about mental health will be about how Gen Z led the charge in creating a culture of true strength not by avoiding discomfort, but by embracing it and growing from it.

GEN Z'S DANGEROUS TENDENCY TO SELFDIAGNOSE VIA SOCIAL MEDIA

Generation Z's embrace of social media as a tool for self-diagnosis represents one of the most troubling cultural shifts we are witnessing today. Platforms like TikTok and Instagram, once intended for entertainment and social connection, have evolved into self-styled mental health clinics only without the training, ethics, or accountability that true healthcare requires. In these chaotic corners of the internet, young people are being exposed to a cascade of misinformation, often provided by individuals with no qualifications, let alone a nuanced understanding of psychology or medical science.

A short, snappy video outlining the supposed "signs" of anxiety, ADHD, or depression can garner millions of views, perpetuating an illusion of authority. These influencers, most of whom have little more than charisma and a cellphone, are offering what can be generously described as superficial assessments of complex mental health conditions. The danger here is that these shallow interpretations not only encourage viewers to adopt labels that do not apply to them but also trivialize what genuine mental health struggles entail. For a generation already grappling with unprecedented levels of anxiety and uncertainty, this tendency to self-diagnoses creates an easy trap an irresistible lure of identity wrapped in a mental health label.

The consequences are severe. By conflating everyday stress or discomfort with clinical disorders, Gen Z is blurring the boundaries between typical human experiences and serious psychological conditions. This leads to overidentification where young people not only see themselves in these disordered descriptors but wear them as badges, creating a new kind of social currency based on suffering. In this climate, mental health is romanticized, almost fetishized, as a means of fitting in or gaining validation. Ironically, instead of breaking down stigma, this overexposure trivializes the lived reality of those who genuinely suffer. The Journal of Adolescent Health warns of the dangerous amplification of these behaviors due to unverified online content, leading to a profound misunderstanding of mental health issues and eroding the legitimacy of true diagnoses.

Perhaps the most pernicious outcome of this trend is the widespread reluctance to seek professional help. If a 15second TikTok can provide a diagnosis, what role do psychologists or psychiatrists play? For many in Gen Z, the idea of consulting an expert becomes unnecessary, even alien. Why pay for an hour with a therapist when an influencer can offer you the same label with the bonus of a comforting community for free? The problem is that this illusion of knowledge and solidarity often prevents those who are genuinely struggling to get the real support they need. Instead, they are given hashtags and virtual likes, when what they desperately need is evidence-based care, understanding, and treatment.

This misguided reliance on social media for health guidance reflects a broader cultural shift towards what I call "DIY Medicine" a dangerous illusion that personal research can replace professional expertise. The ramifications extend beyond mental health; they undermine the very foundation of accountability and responsibility. There is a reason doctors spend years training before they are allowed to diagnose it is a task that requires knowledge, context, and most importantly, a commitment to doing no harm. Generation Z, by turning to influencers for medical insights, has removed those guardrails, opting instead for a crowdsourced version of medicine that is fraught with misinformation and lacking in nuance.

If we are serious about reversing these harmful trends, we must start by challenging Gen Z's reliance on social media as a substitute for genuine expertise. This means fostering a renewed respect for the value of professional consultation and the importance of credible information. It means teaching this generation that identity is not found in a checklist of symptoms, nor in the approval of anonymous followers, but in the hard work of self-discovery, resilience, and growth. Mental health is not a trend and treating it as such is not only ignorant but dangerous. The solution is clear: reject superficial validation, invest in genuine understanding and treatment. Only then can we restore a sense of balance and responsibility to how we view our minds and the challenges they face.

RELIANCE ON MENTAL HEALTH TO AVOID CHALLENGES

The widespread reliance on mental health as an excuse to evade challenges is emblematic of a broader cultural shift away from resilience and toward avoidance. Generation Z has adopted the language of mental health with alarming frequency, transforming what should be a resource for overcoming challenges into a shield to avoid facing them altogether. This trend represents a dangerous departure from traditional values that emphasize perseverance, determination, and the intrinsic reward of overcoming obstacles.

The growing prevalence of "mental health days" in the workplace is a prime example of this dynamic. Employers are increasingly faced with young employees who, rather than managing typical workplace stress, opt out under the guise of selfcare. While it is essential to acknowledge genuine cases of burnout, the ease with which mental health is invoked to justify disengagement from responsibilities is troubling. Stress, pressure, and adversity are inherent aspects of any meaningful endeavor elements that previous generations faced head-on as they built businesses, raised families, and forged communities. The frequent use of mental health to withdraw has made it difficult to differentiate between genuine and insincere claims.

In academic settings, this pattern is even more pronounced. College campuses, which once served as crucibles for intellectual challenge and personal growth, have increasingly become environments where discomfort is avoided at all costs. Many students are not only seeking mental health accommodation as a last resort but are often using them as a default response to the slightest hint of stress or difficulty. Instead of confronting challenges head-on facing the difficult professor, completing the demanding assignment, or dealing with social anxieties many students are retreating into a bubble of perceived safety. This response does not foster growth;

instead, it perpetuates a cycle of dependency that leaves individuals ill-equipped to handle the inevitable pressures of adulthood.

The consequences of this avoidance mindset extend far beyond the individual level. By prioritizing the avoidance of discomfort over the pursuit of resilience, Gen Z risks undermining the very foundations of what it means to be a functioning, contributing member of society. The narrative has shifted from "how can I overcome this?" to "how can I be protected from this?" This approach fosters weakness rather than strength, complacency rather than courage.

The world does not cater to fragility. Progress demands individuals willing to face discomfort, embrace adversity, and prioritize selfcare for resilience. The relentless pursuit of comfort is not the mark of a healthy society; it is a symptom of cultural decay.

True resilience, the kind that built the backbone of earlier generations cannot be developed in an environment where every challenge is deemed too daunting, every discomfort too unbearable. Resilience is forged in the fire of hardship, and it is through facing, not avoiding, these challenges that character is built. Dependence on mental health can hinder the ability to cope with real-world demands. Mental health should empower us to face challenges, not avoid them.

DATA: THE MENTAL HEALTH CRISIS IN GEN Z

The mental health crisis in Gen Z is a symptom of a generation that has been conditioned to prioritize comfort over resilience, validation over transformation. The COVID19 pandemic acted as an accelerant to a fire that was already smoldering, exposing the deep fractures in the mental and emotional constitution of this generation. Gen Z's high levels of anxiety, depression, and loneliness during the pandemic highlight their struggle with adversity.

What makes this crisis even more alarming is not merely the prevalence of mental health issues as those exist across every generation, but Gen Z's collective response to these challenges. Rather than seeking professional help or adopting strategies that could foster real change, many opted for the short-lived solace found in social media communities. These echo chambers offered temporary balm: likes, comments, a fleeting sense of camaraderie but ultimately served as crutches that only deepened their fragility. Social media has become the digital therapist, doling out affirmations and catchy slogans, while real, tangible help remains sidelined.

This choice reflects a broader cultural phenomenon within Gen Z and an aversion to anything that doesn't immediately offer comfort or that challenges their sense of self. The preference for online reassurance over professional advice highlights a growing intolerance for discomfort. True mental health care often requires confronting uncomfortable truths, examining one's habits, and making difficult changes. But Gen Z, raised in an environment that increasingly coddles and shields them from adversity, is more inclined to seek out the comfort of validation over the discomfort of transformation.

This behavior results in a generation paralyzed by fear, stress, and anxiety, unable to engage in solutions. Mental health professionals report frustration over the lack of follow-through from younger patients, who often expect immediate results without the corresponding effort. This mentality is both a product and a perpetuator of fragility. The unwillingness to push through discomfort is setting up a dangerous precedent one where the answer to pain is avoidance, and the path to healing is never embarked upon because it appears too steep or too uncomfortable.

There's no question that mental health issues deserve empathy and attention. But empathy without accountability is simply enabling. Gen Z needs to understand that real progress doesn't come from staying in the warm embrace of sympathetic online communities that reinforce the status quo. It comes from stepping out of that comfort zone and confronting the issues head-on, with professional guidance, a willingness to change, and a commitment to build resilience. Let's empower Gen Z to reclaim their mental health through active participation in the messy and uncomfortable healing process.

Ultimately, this is about redefining strength for an entire generation. True strength is not found in the number of followers who validate your pain, but in the grit to address it, to overcome it, and to grow from it. It is time for Gen Z to stop avoiding the hard road because while comfort is a temporary escape, resilience is the only true path to lasting mental wellbeing.

VICTIMHOOD CULTURE: THE COMFORT OF FRAGILITY

The overemphasis on mental health awareness in recent years has contributed to the rise of a broader "victimhood culture," where individuals derive validation from their struggles rather than striving to overcome them. What began as a much-needed effort to destigmatize mental health has, in many ways, transformed into an unhealthy glorification of fragility. For many, being perceived as vulnerable or fragile has become more rewarding than putting in the hard work required to build resilience and strength. In this victimhood culture, weakness is glorified while strength is often dismissed or even punished, creating an environment where individuals are celebrated for their vulnerabilities and actively discouraged from demonstrating toughness or fortitude.

Jonathan Haidt, in his book The Coddling of the American Mind, discusses how this glorification of fragility leads to a society where resilience is no longer valued. In a culture that prizes comfort and safety over struggle and perseverance, individuals are encouraged to embrace their fragility as a core aspect of their identity. Mental health struggles, rather than being seen as obstacles to overcome, become a defining feature of one's identity — a badge of authenticity and worth. This has serious consequences for the individual, as these struggles become difficult to shed, not just because of their intrinsic difficulty, but because overcoming them would mean losing the validation that comes from others. For many, there is an unspoken incentive to remain in a state of vulnerability, as moving beyond it might lead to a loss of attention, support, or perceived value.

The influence of social media on this phenomenon cannot be overstated. Platforms like TikTok have amplified the culture of victimhood, providing a massive audience for users who share their personal struggles. Mental health videos often receive significant praise and validation, with users being encouraged to embrace and showcase their fragility. While the intention may be to create a supportive environment, the unintended consequence is the promotion of vulnerability over growth. Rather than offering messages of empowerment — encouraging individuals to seek strength, resilience, and recovery, these platforms often promote a cycle of fragility, where the emphasis is on embracing one's weaknesses without any movement toward overcoming them.

Take, for example, the trend on TikTok where young users openly diagnose themselves with serious mental health conditions like anxiety, depression, or even more complex disorders such as dissociative identity disorder (DID). Many of these self-diagnoses are made without any professional input, yet these individuals receive overwhelming praise from viewers for their "bravery" in speaking about their struggles. This dynamic fosters an environment where identity is closely tied to mental health issues, making it even more challenging for individuals to move beyond them. For Generation Z, a generation raised in an online world where validation is currency, the constant reinforcement of these struggles can lead to an entrenched sense of victimhood that prevents genuine personal growth.

The issue is not the acknowledgment of mental health struggles—indeed, raising awareness and providing support are critically important. The problem lies in the cultural shift toward valuing vulnerability to such an extent that it becomes preferable to strength. There is a difference between creating an environment that supports those with mental health struggles and creating a culture that celebrates fragility as a permanent state of being. When fragility becomes glorified, resilience and the courage to overcome challenges are viewed as less important or even undesirable. This mindset is detrimental, not only to the individual but to society. It leads to a population that is less capable of dealing with adversity, less willing to take risks, and ultimately less prepared to face the inevitable challenges of life.

This culture of fragility extends beyond individual mental health and has permeated educational institutions and workplaces. Universities, which should be places where young people are challenged to grow and to confront uncomfortable ideas, have increasingly embraced policies that prioritize emotional comfort over resilience. Trigger warnings, safe spaces, and the avoidance of potentially upsetting content are all manifestations of this broader victimhood culture. While originally intended to provide a supportive learning environment, these measures have often been taken to an extreme, where students are shielded from any form of discomfort. This approach not only undermines the purpose of education but also leaves students ill-equipped to deal with the complexities of the real world—a world that does not come with trigger warnings or safe spaces.

The effects of this culture can also be seen in the workforce, where young employees increasingly expect their employers to cater to their emotional needs in ways that go beyond traditional workplace accommodations. There have been numerous reports of companies struggling with the demands of younger employees who expect their work environment to reflect the same kind of emotional protection that they experienced in school. This includes expectations for emotional validation, an avoidance of challenging feedback, and a work culture that prioritizes comfort over productivity and growth. Such expectations are a direct reflection of the broader victimhood culture that celebrates fragility over resilience. They reflect a fundamental misunderstanding of the realities of the professional world, where success often requires individuals to step outside their comfort zones, to take risks, and to handle constructive criticism.

The media has played a role in fostering this culture as well. Mainstream media outlets frequently spotlight personal stories of struggle, focusing on the vulnerabilities of individuals in ways that often glamorize their suffering. The narrative tends to be one of validation rather than one of empowerment—individuals are celebrated for their struggles, but there is rarely a focus on how they can, or did, overcome these challenges. This narrative can be particularly damaging because it creates the perception that one's worth is intrinsically tied to being a victim. It sends a message that staying in a state of struggle is preferable to overcoming it because that is where the attention, sympathy, and support are found.

Consider the rise in popularity of the term "emotional labor," which has become a way for individuals to frame any kind of emotional discomfort as a form of undue burden. The concept originally referred to the legitimate challenges faced by service workers who had to manage their emotions as part of their jobs. However, it has since been coopted to describe virtually any interpersonal interaction that causes discomfort. This shift reflects a broader cultural reluctance to deal with the normal challenges of human relationships and a preference for framing oneself as a victim of even the most routine emotional experiences. It is another example of how the culture of victimhood has expanded to encompass every aspect of life, encouraging people to see themselves as fragile and oppressed rather than as capable and resilient.

The long-term implications of this mindset are concerning. A society that glorifies fragility over strength is one that is ill-prepared to face adversity. Challenges, both personal and societal, require resilience, courage, and the ability to persevere in the face of obstacles. If individuals are conditioned to view themselves as fragile, if they are rewarded for staying in a state of vulnerability rather than encouraged to overcome it, then they are less likely to develop the skills and the mindset necessary to confront life's challenges. This does not only impact individual wellbeing; it impacts society's capacity to innovate, to adapt, and to thrive.

Generation Z is at risk of falling into this trap. Raised in a world where social media platforms like TikTok and Instagram reward vulnerability with likes, shares, and validation, many members of this generation have internalized the belief that their worth is tied to their struggles. They see their peers gaining attention and support by sharing their mental health battles and are encouraged to do the same. This creates a feedback loop where vulnerability is not just expressed but is performed, and where the goal becomes not overcoming challenges but maintaining them as a source of identity and validation. This mindset is fundamentally at odds with the concept of personal growth, which requires individuals to confront their weaknesses, to push past them, and to emerge stronger on the other side.

If we are to counter this trend, we must shift the narrative away from glorifying fragility and toward celebrating resilience. Mental health awareness is important, but it must be balanced with a focus on empowerment and recovery. We need to create environments, both online and offline, that support individuals in their struggles while also encouraging them to move beyond them. This means valuing strength, perseverance, and the ability to overcome adversity. It means recognizing that while vulnerability is a part of the human experience, it is not the end goal—growth, strength, and resilience are.

The culture of victimhood is not just a cultural fad; it is a deeply ingrained mindset that has far-reaching implications for society. By glorifying vulnerability and punishing strength, we are creating a population that is less prepared to face the inevitable challenges of life. We are discouraging personal growth, stifling resilience, and ultimately weakening the fabric of our society. To truly support mental health, we must encourage individuals not only to speak about their struggles but to strive to overcome them. We must celebrate those who, despite their hardships, choose to rise, to fight, and to grow. Only by doing so can we hope to foster a culture that values resilience over fragility, strength over victimhood, and growth over stagnation.

AVOIDING CHALLENGES

The glorification of fragility has far-reaching implications that extend well beyond individual wellbeing; it affects our educational systems, workplace environments, and overall societal resilience. The elevation of vulnerability over strength has resulted in an environment where avoiding challenges is seen as both acceptable and even commendable. This trend not only hinders personal growth but also risks creating a generation that is ill-equipped to face the realities of adult life.

In schools, the impact of this cultural shift is increasingly evident. Students today are often given the option to opt out of challenging courses, projects, or exams under the guise of protecting their mental health. While it is critical that schools take mental health seriously, the problem arises when mental health is used as a catchall justification for avoiding discomfort, challenge, or hard work. For instance, students who find advanced mathematics or science courses too demanding are often allowed to withdraw without any expectation to work through their struggles. Instead of being encouraged to tackle these challenges and develop coping skills, students are given an easy way out. This avoidance might provide temporary relief, but it ultimately does disservice to the students. By sidestepping these hurdles, they are deprived of the opportunity to build resilience and confidence — traits that can only be developed by pushing through difficulties.

The idea that students should always be protected from stress or pressure has become a dominant narrative, and this mindset has extended into university settings as well. Trigger warnings, the proliferation of "safe spaces," and policies that prioritize emotional comfort over intellectual challenge are now commonplace on many college campuses. These measures were originally introduced to create a more inclusive learning environment, but they have often been taken to extremes, resulting in an educational atmosphere that prizes comfort over growth. Universities should be places where young adults are challenged to expand their thinking, confront new ideas, and develop the intellectual toughness required to engage with the world. Instead, many universities have created environments where students are shielded from any potential discomfort, thus stunting their intellectual and emotional development.

The consequences of this victimhood culture do not end in academia; they follow individuals into the workplace as well. The first wave of Generation Z is now entering the workforce, bringing with them expectations shaped by years of accommodation in educational environments. Increasingly, young employees are demanding accommodation in the workplace that go well beyond the legal requirements set forth to ensure a safe and fair work environment. They expect their jobs to be stress-free and are often unwilling to take on tasks that might push them out of their comfort zones. When confronted with the inevitable pressures of work — deadlines, constructive criticism, or challenging projects, many young employees are quick to cite mental health as a reason to avoid these situations.

There have been numerous reports from employers struggling to manage these expectations. Managers are often faced with young employees who believe they should be exempt from any situation that might cause stress, regardless of the nature of the job. This mindset is particularly concerning industries where high pressure and the ability to cope with stress are inherent parts of the job, such as healthcare, finance, or law. Employers are finding it increasingly difficult to strike a balance between supporting employee wellbeing and ensuring that work gets done efficiently and effectively. The expectation that work should always be emotionally comfortable is unrealistic and ultimately harmful, as it prevents young employees from developing the resilience and grit that are necessary for career advancement and success.

Consider the tech industry, where a significant portion of the workforce is comprised of younger employees. Companies like Google and Facebook have implemented extensive wellness programs, complete with nap pods, stress relief zones, and emotional support animals. While these initiatives are well-intentioned, aiming to support employee wellbeing, they also reinforce the notion that individuals should be protected from all stressors. This has contributed to a culture where resilience is undervalued, and where any form of adversity is seen as something to be avoided rather than confronted. While promoting wellbeing is important, the unintended consequence of these practices is the reinforcement of a fragile workforce—one that is less capable of dealing with setbacks, criticism, or pressure.

This cultural aversion to stress and challenge is not just affecting individuals in their academic and professional lives, it is weakening society. A culture that glorifies fragility and promotes the avoidance of discomfort is one that ultimately lacks resilience. Life is inherently challenging, filled with setbacks, uncertainties, and hardships. The only way to navigate these difficulties effectively is to develop coping mechanisms, resilience, and strength—all of which require experiencing, and overcoming, adversity. By fostering an environment where individuals are encouraged to avoid challenges rather than face them head-on, we are setting them up for failure in the real world, where problems cannot simply be opted out of.

Moreover, the glorification of fragility has led to a widespread rejection of personal accountability. In a culture that celebrates victimhood, individuals are often encouraged to attribute their difficulties to external factors, be it systemic oppression, workplace dynamics, or other people — rather than taking personal responsibility for their circumstances. This mindset discourages individuals from seeking constructive ways to overcome their challenges, fostering a sense of helplessness instead. The ability to assess one's own role in a situation, to learn from failures, and to grow as a result, is fundamental to personal development. When the narrative becomes one of perpetual victimhood, the incentive to make proactive changes is diminished, replaced instead by the expectation that others should change to accommodate one's needs.

This culture of fragility also has significant implications for interpersonal relationships. Friendships, familial bonds, and romantic partnerships all require resilience, patience, and the ability to navigate conflict. However, a culture that promotes fragility over toughness is one that is increasingly ill-equipped to handle the inevitable challenges that come with human relationships. Disagreements are seen as threats, differing opinions are viewed as personal attacks, and emotional discomfort becomes a justification for cutting people off. The rise of terms like "toxic" to describe any relationship that involves conflict, discomfort, or growth challenges is a testament to how deeply ingrained the avoidance of adversity has become. Instead of working through difficulties, many individuals are quick to end relationships altogether, believing that discomfort is inherently harmful rather than an opportunity for growth.

For Generation Z, growing up in this culture of glorified fragility has meant being conditioned to believe that avoiding challenges is both acceptable and desirable. They have been raised in environments where emotional comfort is prioritized above all else, where resilience is rarely celebrated, and where the response to adversity is often to avoid or eliminate it. As a result, many members of this generation are entering adulthood without the tools necessary to cope with the realities of life, which are often uncomfortable, unpredictable, and challenging. The glorification of fragility has left them vulnerable, unprepared, and lacking the resilience that is crucial for navigating the complexities of adult life.

The long-term effects of this mindset are profound. Individuals who have not developed resilience are less capable of dealing with personal setbacks, professional challenges, or societal issues. They are more likely to experience mental health problems, not because they have faced too many challenges, but because they have faced too few and therefore lack the coping mechanisms necessary to navigate adversity. The glorification of fragility has created a paradox: in our efforts to protect individuals from discomfort and challenge, we have made them more vulnerable to the very struggles we sought to shield them from.

To counter this trend, society must shift its focus from glorifying vulnerability to celebrating resilience. It is not enough to simply be aware of one's mental health struggles; we must also encourage individuals to actively seek ways to overcome them. Schools need to push students to engage with challenging subjects, even if it makes them uncomfortable. Universities should create environments where debate, challenge, and intellectual struggle are seen as vital parts of the learning process. Workplaces must find a balance between supporting employee wellbeing and challenging them to grow, to take risks, and to face pressure head-on.

Above all, we must reject the narrative that fragility is a virtue. Vulnerability is a part of the human experience, and acknowledging it is important, but it should not be the defining feature of who we are. Strength, resilience, and the ability to overcome adversity — these are the traits that we should aspire to cultivate and celebrate. Only by embracing challenges, by seeing them as opportunities for growth rather than threats to be avoided, can we build a society that is resilient, capable, and prepared to face whatever challenges the future holds. It is time to move away from the culture of glorified fragility and to foster a culture that values strength, perseverance, and the willingness to confront life's inevitable challenges with courage and determination.

CONNECTION TO DECLINE: FROM VICTIMHOOD TO DEPENDENCE

The current focus on victimhood and fragility is not occurring in isolation; it mirrors a broader societal trend toward dependence that has been developing for decades. Just as earlier generations became increasingly reliant on welfare programs and government assistance, today's young adults are increasingly leaning on mental health diagnoses and a culture of vulnerability as a means to avoid personal responsibility. This shift reflects an underlying mentality where dependence is not just tolerated—it is encouraged, and in many cases, it is glorified. Individual agency, the concept that people have the power and responsibility to shape their own lives, is increasingly seen as too burdensome to bear. This attitude threatens the core values that have historically defined personal and community resilience.

The erosion of personal agency is perhaps the most troubling aspect of this trend. When individuals use mental health struggles as a reason to avoid challenges, they deny themselves the opportunity to grow. Coping mechanisms are not inherent; they are developed through experience, particularly through the process of confronting and overcoming obstacles. By choosing to lean into fragility and avoid difficulties, individuals are missing out on crucial opportunities to develop the grit and perseverance that are necessary for real growth and maturity. This trend is especially concerning for Generation Z, who have grown up in a world that increasingly values emotional comfort over resilience. The grit and determination that defined previous generations—who built communities, businesses, and families under often incredibly challenging circumstances—are being replaced by a culture that views discomfort as trauma and challenges as inherently harmful.

The glorification of dependence is not only evident in the personal lives of individuals but also in how society at large is structured. Government programs that were originally designed to act as safety nets have evolved into permanent fixtures of dependence for large segments of the population. While these programs have undoubtedly provided essential support for those in genuine need, there is a significant difference between a temporary safety net and a permanent way of life. Today's version of liberalism, with its emphasis on entitlement over empowerment, encourages a mentality where people feel they are owed comfort, financial stability, and emotional validation, regardless of their efforts or actions. This mindset fosters a cycle of dependence, where individuals look outward for solutions rather than inward, diminishing the sense of agency that is crucial for self-improvement and societal contribution.

Consider the recent rise in the number of young adults who are choosing to live at home with their parents well into their late twenties and even thirties. While economic challenges certainly play a role in this trend, there is also an element of unwillingness to face the discomfort that comes with independent living. Moving out, managing finances, paying bills, and dealing with the pressures of adulthood are daunting, but they are also necessary steps in building resilience and self-reliance. Instead, we are seeing a growing number of young adults choosing to remain in the safety and comfort of their parents' homes, avoiding the struggles and challenges that are an essential part of the maturation process. This trend further illustrates how dependence is becoming the default, and the concept of taking personal control over one's life is becoming increasingly rare.

Social media, once again, plays a significant role in reinforcing this dependence. Platforms like TikTok and Instagram have become virtual stages where individuals can showcase their vulnerabilities and receive praise for their struggles. While this can create a sense of community and shared experience, it also encourages the commodification of personal struggles. Mental health issues are often framed in ways that garner sympathy and validation, but without a corresponding emphasis on solutions, resilience, or overcoming these challenges. Instead of encouraging personal growth, social media platforms often provide an audience that rewards the status quo—where staying in a state of struggle becomes more socially rewarding than the hard, often solitary work of growth and recovery.

A notable example of this is the rise of self-diagnosis on platforms like TikTok, where young people attribute their behavior or emotions to serious mental health conditions such as depression, anxiety, or ADHD. These self-diagnoses are then shared with an audience that provides positive reinforcement, validating the individual's experience without necessarily encouraging them to seek professional help or consider strategies for improvement. The result is a culture that celebrates the identification with a struggle but has little interest in the process of overcoming it. It is a culture where dependence on a diagnosis becomes a form of identity—a badge of authenticity that discourages growth and independence. This dynamic is problematic because it turns mental health into a form of social currency, rather than something to be addressed and managed in the pursuit of a healthier, more independent life.

The workplace, too, has been affected by this trend toward dependence and fragility. Employers are increasingly faced with young employees who expect not only accommodation but a work environment that shields them from all forms of stress and discomfort. The expectation is that jobs should cater to the emotional needs of the individual, rather than the individual adapting to the demands of the job. This is reflected in the growing popularity of concepts like "quiet quitting," where employees do the bare minimum required of them, often framing it as a form of selfcare. While it is crucial to avoid burnout and maintain a healthy work-life balance, there is also a danger in normalizing avoidance as a primary coping strategy. The reality is that work is often challenging, and success in any field requires the ability to endure stress, face obstacles, and grow through adversity. By glorifying avoidance and dependence, we are eroding the values of hard work, perseverance, and accountability that are essential for personal and professional success.

In the past, communities were built on the values of hard work, sacrifice, and resilience. Individuals understood that facing challenges head-on was part of contributing to something greater than themselves, whether it was providing for their families, building businesses, or supporting their neighbors. Today, however, these values are increasingly being replaced by a mentality that prioritizes comfort over contribution. The concept of "selfcare" has been distorted to the point where it is often used as an excuse to avoid anything difficult or uncomfortable. While selfcare is undeniably important, when it becomes an excuse to avoid challenges, it loses its value and becomes yet another form of dependence — a way to opt out of the demands of life rather than a means to recharge to meet those demands effectively.

The broader implications of this culture of dependence and fragility are profound. A society that discourages personal agency and glorifies victimhood is one that is less capable of innovation, less capable of overcoming adversity, and ultimately less capable of thriving. The values that once built strong communities—hard work, sacrifice, resilience, and personal responsibility—are being eroded by a mentality that sees discomfort as inherently harmful and dependence as a virtue. Without the experience of overcoming adversity, individuals do not develop the coping skills necessary for real growth. The grit, determination, and perseverance that defined earlier generations are being lost, replaced by a culture that values comfort over courage and avoidance over action.

If society is to reclaim the values that lead to strength and independence, there must be a shift in how we view personal agency and responsibility. Mental health awareness is critical, but it should not come at the expense of resilience and self-reliance. Encouraging individuals to face challenges, to push through discomfort, and to take control of their own lives is not being insensitive—it is empowering. Schools must encourage students to confront difficult subjects and to persevere in the face of failure. Workplaces must balance accommodations with expectations, providing support while also fostering an environment where resilience and growth are prioritized.

Most importantly, as a culture, we must move away from glorifying dependence and victimhood and toward celebrating strength, resilience, and the pursuit of independence. True empowerment does not come from avoiding challenges; it comes from facing them, from struggling, and from growing as a result. It comes from understanding that while life is often difficult, individuals have the power and responsibility to shape their own destinies. By shifting our focus back to these values, we can begin to rebuild a culture that values independence over dependence, strength over fragility, and resilience over avoidance. Only then can we hope to foster individuals—and communities—that are truly capable of thriving in the face of life's inevitable challenges.

BUILDING RESILIENCE

If there is a way out of this downward spiral, it lies in reclaiming personal agency and fostering resilience. The current narrative around mental health awareness, while well-intentioned, has been twisted into something that often provides a shield to hide behind rather than a foundation from which individuals can grow stronger. True mental health awareness should be about empowering individuals, helping them build a foundation of strength, and teaching them that struggle is a part of life that can be overcome, not a defining limitation. It must be about fostering resilience, not providing an excuse for dependency or withdrawal. Generation Z must shift this narrative if we hope to cultivate a healthier and stronger society.

The conversation surrounding mental health must be reframed entirely. Instead of viewing mental health as a label that defines a person or a reason to avoid discomfort, it should be framed as an opportunity for growth—a challenge to be faced and ultimately a pathway to empowerment. Life is inherently filled with obstacles and adversities, and mental health struggles are no different from any other form of hardship. Just as one would train their body to overcome physical challenges, individuals must be encouraged to train their minds to overcome emotional and psychological challenges. Mental health, therefore, should not be synonymous with vulnerability or fragility; it should represent an area for personal development, where individuals can strengthen their capacity to cope, adapt, and ultimately thrive.

For Gen Z, who have grown up immersed in the culture of social media validation and the glorification of vulnerability, this shift is particularly crucial. They need to understand that while it is okay to seek support and to express struggles, true empowerment comes from pushing through those struggles and not allowing them to define one's life. TikTok, Instagram, and other social media platforms should not simply be places where people gather to share their struggles, but also spaces where they celebrate their victories—where they share stories of resilience, overcoming fears, and conquering challenges. Instead of accumulating likes and shares for identifying with a struggle, young people need to be praised for their efforts to rise above these struggles. The narrative needs to pivot away from glorifying the status of being a victim and instead celebrate those who overcome, who grow stronger in the face of adversity.

The celebration of fragility must be rejected. This does not mean we should ignore the very real mental health struggles that people face. It means that rather than glorifying these struggles as something that gives one intrinsic value, we need to celebrate the ability to face adversity head-on, the courage to confront challenges, and the perseverance that allows individuals to emerge stronger. Instead of embracing a narrative that turns vulnerability into a permanent state of being, we need to promote resilience and the willingness to face discomfort, to learn, and to grow. Resilience is not about denying one's struggles; it is about acknowledging them, confronting them, and refusing to be defined by them.

The current narrative has taken the concept of mental health support and turned it into a culture of dependency, where struggles are treated as reasons to withdraw rather than challenges to overcome. Mental health support should be about equipping individuals with the tools they need to thrive, teaching them coping strategies, and helping them understand that they are capable of more than they may realize. Therapy, counseling, and support networks should empower individuals to face their fears and overcome obstacles, not encourage them to retreat from anything that causes discomfort. The role of mental health professionals should be to guide individuals on a path toward resilience and independence, fostering an understanding that while support is valuable, true strength comes from within.

In educational institutions, we must change how mental health is approached. Instead of allowing students to opt out of challenges in the name of protecting mental health, schools should offer tools and support systems that help students rise to meet those challenges. Stress management workshops, resilience training, and opportunities for students to safely face and overcome fears are all crucial. The message should not be that challenges are something to be avoided, but that they are something to be faced and conquered with the right support. Universities, too, should prioritize intellectual challenge and growth, providing environments where young people learn to navigate discomfort, handle opposing viewpoints, and engage with difficult subjects. Emotional growth comes from facing, not avoiding, the things that make us uncomfortable.

In the workplace, mental health accommodations should not be about eliminating all stress and discomfort. Instead, they should be about creating an environment where employees are supported in facing challenges — where there are resources to help them manage stress, but also an expectation that they will push through adversity, take on difficult tasks, and grow from the experience. Resilience training programs, mentorship, and opportunities for personal development should be integral parts of workplace mental health initiatives. Employers must find a way to balance support with the expectation of performance and growth, creating a culture that values perseverance over avoidance.

Social media also has a role to play in shifting this narrative. Influencers and content creators, who wield significant influence over the younger generation, should be encouraged to share not only their struggles but also their journeys toward overcoming them. The focus should be on the solutions, the tools, and the processes that helped them grow stronger. Stories of personal triumph, of facing fears, of building resilience — these are the stories that need to be amplified, rather than the endless glorification of victimhood. The algorithms that prioritize emotional vulnerability need to be recalibrated to reward growth, resilience, and strength.

Platforms like TikTok should be filled with examples of young people taking on challenges, stepping out of their comfort zones, and succeeding—not just with stories of emotional pain left unresolved.

The media must also play its part. Instead of focusing solely on stories of struggle, mainstream media should highlight stories of recovery, of resilience, and of growth. Stories that show people who faced immense challenges and came out stronger on the other side need to be given more airtime. The message needs to shift away from "it's okay to struggle" to "it's okay to struggle, and here is how you can overcome it." Empowerment should be the focus—not the glorification of remaining in a state of struggle.

For Gen Z and society to move forward, we must fundamentally change how we think about mental health, vulnerability, and resilience. Struggles are a part of the human condition, but they are not what define us. What defines us is how we respond to these struggles. It is the courage to confront them, the strength to persevere, and the resilience to grow that truly matters. The narrative around mental health must become one of empowerment. We must teach young people that while it is okay to be vulnerable, it is even better to be strong, to face adversity, and to build the kind of mental toughness that will serve them throughout their lives.

The glorification of fragility and the culture of victimhood have led us down a dangerous path—one where dependence is seen as acceptable, and individual agency is increasingly viewed as a burden. If we are to break free from this cycle of dependence and decline, we must reject this glorification. We need to redefine what it means to be strong, to be capable, and to be resilient. Mental health support must be about equipping individuals with the tools they need to face the world, not providing excuses for them to retreat from it. It must be about helping people find the strength within themselves, empowering them to confront their fears, and ultimately grow stronger as a result.

Only then can we hope to build a society that values strength, growth, and true mental wellness. A society where individuals are not defined by their struggles but by their ability to overcome them. A society that celebrates resilience, that fosters independence, and that encourages every person to reach their full potential. By reclaiming personal agency, fostering resilience, and rejecting the glorification of fragility, we can create a future that is not only stronger but more hopeful—a future where individuals and communities alike are empowered to face whatever challenges come their way.

CHAPTER FIVE

RESILIENCE IN DECLINE

The erosion of resilience in modern society is a topic of growing concern, particularly when examining generational trends. Over time, society's perception of what constitutes strength, toughness, and the ability to endure hardship has changed dramatically, resulting in a steady decline in resilience, especially in younger generations. This chapter explores the generational decline in resilience and toughness, utilizing examples from military training and university environments to illustrate how modern societal shifts have placed an undue emphasis on comfort and safety at the expense of grit and endurance. By contrasting today's emphasis on emotional protection with the experiences of the Greatest Generation, who weathered the Great Depression and fought in World War II, we can better understand how modern approaches to mental health, physical toughness, and emotional resilience have fundamentally weakened our ability to face challenges head-on.

The Greatest Generation was defined by its resilience. These were individuals who grew up in the throes of the Great Depression, enduring poverty, economic hardship, and uncertainty. When the world plunged into global conflict, they were called to fight in World War II, facing unimaginable horrors and hardships. They emerged as victors not just because of military might, but because of their collective resilience, their willingness to endure, and their understanding that adversity, no matter how daunting, must be faced with strength and perseverance. This resilience reflected their times; hardship was not something to be feared or avoided, but a reality that shaped their character and made them stronger.

Fast forward to today, and we see a stark contrast in how society approaches adversity. Resilience, once seen as a vital trait, has been overshadowed by an emphasis on emotional protection and a desire to eliminate discomfort at all costs. This shift is evident in the way we approach education and training environments — spaces that are supposed to prepare individuals to face the real world but have increasingly become incubators of fragility.

Consider the changes that have taken place in military training. Historically, military boot camps broke down recruits and built them back up as resilient, cohesive units prepared to face the harsh realities of combat. The goal was not only to develop physical toughness but also to foster mental resilience and the ability to persevere under extreme conditions. Today, military training has been softened in response to modern sensibilities about mental health and emotional wellbeing. In some branches, practices that were once deemed essential for fostering resilience are now seen as unnecessarily harsh or even abusive. Introducing "stress cards" during boot camp — a card that recruits can present when they feel too stressed to continue — is a striking example of how the expectations for toughness have changed. Rather than teaching recruits how to manage and overcome stress, the emphasis has shifted toward accommodating it, creating a pathway for individuals to opt out of discomfort.

The effects of this shift are concerning. Military service is demanding and often traumatic. The battlefield does not offer safe spaces, and stress cards do not exist in actual combat. By prioritizing emotional comfort over resilience in training, we are failing to adequately prepare soldiers for the realities they will face. The intention behind these changes may be to protect recruits' mental health, but the unintended consequence is a reduction in their ability to handle the intense pressures of warfare. It is not about being needlessly harsh; it is about preparing individuals for the most extreme situations imaginable, where the ability to remain calm under pressure, to endure hardship, and to push through fear can mean the difference between life and death.

The erosion of resilience is also evident in university environments. Colleges and universities were once places where young adults were challenged intellectually, emotionally, and physically. They were places where ideas clashed, where students were encouraged to think critically, to question their beliefs, and to engage with those who held opposing viewpoints. Today, many universities have shifted away from this model, choosing instead to prioritize emotional protection over intellectual challenge. Trigger warnings, safe spaces, and the avoidance of potentially upsetting content have become commonplace. While these practices were initially introduced to create a more inclusive and supportive environment, they have often been taken to extremes, resulting in an educational atmosphere that prizes comfort over growth.

When students are shielded from ideas or experiences that might make them uncomfortable, they miss out on opportunities to develop resilience. Confronting challenging or upsetting ideas is a crucial part of the educational process—it is how students learn to think critically, to defend their beliefs, and to understand the perspectives of others. By avoiding these challenges, universities are producing graduates who are intellectually fragile, unable to cope with ideas that conflict with their worldview, and unprepared for the complexities of the real world, where disagreement and discomfort are inevitable. The idea that students need to be protected from anything that might upset them not only undermines the purpose of education but also robs them of the chance to develop the resilience they will need throughout their lives.

The contrast between the Greatest Generation and today's young adults highlights just how much our values have shifted. The Greatest Generation faced adversity head-on, understanding that hardship was an unavoidable part of life that could be overcome through perseverance, grit, and community support. Modern society, however, has become increasingly focused on the idea that individuals must be protected from all forms of discomfort, that safety and emotional wellbeing should take precedence over all else. This mentality is reflected not only in how we approach military training and education but also in the broader societal narrative around mental health and wellbeing.

Mental health, once a topic shrouded in stigma, has thankfully become a more open subject of discussion. However, the way we discuss mental health has also contributed to the decline in resilience. Mental health awareness today often emphasizes the avoidance of stress and discomfort rather than the development of coping mechanisms. The narrative is one of fragility, where individuals are encouraged to see themselves as vulnerable, in need of protection from the world around them. This framing, while well-intentioned, ultimately undermines the development of resilience. Instead of encouraging individuals to build the strength needed to navigate life's inevitable challenges, it promotes a dependence on external validation and protection. Mental health awareness should be about equipping people with the tools to grow stronger, to manage their struggles effectively, and to become more resilient—not about encouraging them to avoid challenges altogether.

The cultural shift toward comfort and safety has profound implications for society at large. A population that is not resilient, that has not developed the ability to endure and overcome hardship, is ill-prepared to face the collective challenges that inevitably arise. Whether it is a global pandemic, economic uncertainty, or the threat of conflict, societies require individuals who are capable of facing adversity without crumbling. The Greatest Generation understood this intuitively. They lived through some of the most challenging times in modern history, and their resilience was a key factor in their ability to rebuild and thrive after the devastation of World War II. Today, however, we are at risk of losing these crucial qualities. The emphasis on emotional protection, the glorification of fragility, and the avoidance of discomfort are creating a society that is less prepared to face the challenges of the future.

If there is a way to reverse this trend, it lies in a fundamental shift in how we think about adversity, resilience, and growth. We need to move away from the idea that individuals must be protected from every form of discomfort and instead embrace the notion that challenges are opportunities for growth. Military training should once again focus on building the mental toughness that is necessary for combat. Universities should be places where students are exposed to challenging ideas, where they are encouraged to think critically and engage deeply with topics that may make them uncomfortable. Mental health awareness should not be about avoiding stress, but about learning how to manage it effectively, about developing the resilience to thrive even in the face of adversity.

We must also change the way we talk about success and achievement. The Greatest Generation did not see themselves as victims of their circumstances; they saw themselves as survivors, as individuals capable of overcoming whatever life threw at them. This mindset needs to be cultivated in younger generations. Instead of glorifying vulnerability and celebrating fragility, we need to celebrate strength, perseverance, and the ability to overcome challenges. This does not mean ignoring mental health issues or denying the importance of emotional wellbeing — it means recognizing that true wellbeing comes from the confidence that one can face and overcome hardship, not from avoiding it.

Resilience is not an inherent trait — it is something that must be developed, cultivated, and practiced. It requires facing fears, taking risks, and stepping outside of one's comfort zone. It requires the ability to cope with failure, to learn from setbacks, and to keep moving forward even when things get tough. If we continue down the path of prioritizing comfort and safety over resilience and toughness, we risk creating a society that is not only fragile but also unable to face the inevitable challenges of the future. By reclaiming the values of grit, determination, and perseverance, we can begin to reverse this decline in resilience and build a generation that is prepared to face whatever comes their way with strength and courage.

THE EVOLUTION OF MILITARY TRAINING: FROM BOOT CAMP TO STRESS CARDS

Military training has long been defined by its intensity, rigor, and purpose: to forge resilient soldiers capable of withstanding the hardships of war. Historically, boot camp was a crucible, designed to strip away individual weaknesses and build physical endurance, mental toughness, and emotional resilience. It was, and remains, the first phase in transforming civilians into soldiers—individuals prepared to operate cohesively in the chaotic, high-pressure environments of combat.

However, military training has evolved significantly over the past few decades, reflecting broader societal shifts that emphasize personal wellbeing and emotional protection. These changes are most apparent in the shift from the hardship-oriented boot camp of past generations to modern training programs that incorporate psychological support systems, sometimes at the expense of the toughness that once characterized military readiness. This evolution has sparked debate about whether these adjustments compromise the core purpose of military training: to prepare soldiers for the brutal, unrelenting realities of combat.

THE TRADITIONAL ROLE OF BOOT CAMP: TOUGHNESS AND UNITY

In previous generations, boot camp was synonymous with physical and mental endurance. The objective was to push recruits far beyond their perceived limits, breaking them down to rebuild them into soldiers capable of enduring extreme hardship. The process was brutal but purposeful, simulating the chaos and stress of combat in a controlled environment. Recruits were subjected to grueling physical exercises, relentless discipline, and psychological stressors that aimed to forge resilience. The training process was not about cruelty for its own sake; rather, it was designed to ensure that soldiers could survive and function effectively under the most difficult conditions.

Combat is unpredictable, intense, and unforgiving. To succeed, soldiers must develop the ability to remain calm, focused, and decisive under immense pressure. Boot camp served as a proving ground where recruits were tested physically and mentally, learning to push beyond their limits.

The relentless demands of the training environment not only prepared soldiers for the physical rigors of war but also cultivated a mindset of endurance, discipline, and sacrifice. This process fostered deep bonds of camaraderie among soldiers, as they learned to rely on each other, knowing that their lives could one day depend on the unity forged through shared hardship.

THE SOFTENING OF MILITARY TRAINING

Over time, military training has softened, largely in response to shifting cultural attitudes. A growing emphasis on personal wellbeing and emotional safety has led to changes in the way recruits are trained, with certain aspects of traditional boot camp deemed unnecessarily harsh. Physical demands have been reduced, and psychological support systems, while beneficial for mental health, have been introduced in ways that some argue compromise the intensity of the training experience.

One of the most striking examples of this shift is the rumored introduction of "stress cards," which some branches of the military allegedly distributed to recruits as a way to signal when they felt overwhelmed. While the existence of these cards remains a topic of debate—often dismissed as an urban legend—the concept itself is emblematic of a broader cultural move away from embracing hardship. Rather than being pushed to develop the mental toughness required for combat, recruits were reportedly given the option to step back when things became too difficult.

The underlying intent of stress cards, and similar initiatives, is to protect the mental health of recruits—a goal that, on its own, is laudable. However, critics argue that such measures undermine the core purpose of boot camp. Combat, by its very nature, is stressful and overwhelming, and there are no "stress cards" on the battlefield. Soldiers must be capable of operating under intense pressure without the option to pause or retreat. By softening the demands of boot camp, the military risks producing soldiers who are physically fit but mentally unprepared for the realities of war.

THE IMPACT OF SOCIETAL SHIFTS ON MILITARY READINESS

The softening of military training is part of a broader societal trend that prioritizes emotional comfort and wellbeing over physical and mental toughness. In education, workplaces, and even in how we raise children, there has been a noticeable shift toward avoiding discomfort and minimizing stress. While this approach has certain benefits—particularly in reducing unnecessary harm—its long-term consequences include the erosion of resilience and the loss of the ability to endure hardship.

In the military context, this shift raises critical concerns about preparedness. The nature of warfare has not changed: combat remains as brutal, demanding, and unpredictable as ever. Soldiers must be prepared to face extreme physical exhaustion, psychological strain, and the ever-present possibility of death. If military training prioritizes emotional safety over the development of toughness, soldiers may find themselves unprepared for the harsh realities of war, where there are no accommodations for discomfort.

This cultural shift has also influenced the recruitment pool. Generation Z, the primary demographic now entering military service, is growing up in an era that values comfort and selfcare. Rising rates of obesity, lower physical fitness, and declining academic performance have reduced the number of young people eligible to enlist. Many are simply not meeting the physical or mental standards required for military service. The generation's focus on immediate gratification and work-life balance has also made military service—a career path defined by sacrifice and discipline—less appealing.

THE CONSEQUENCES FOR COMBAT EFFECTIVENESS

The decline in the toughness of military training has far-reaching implications for combat effectiveness. Warfare demands soldiers who can endure prolonged stress, make rapid decisions under pressure, and continue to function when physically and mentally exhausted. Soldiers who have not been pushed to their limits during training may lack the resilience required to survive and succeed in combat. This concern is compounded by studies from the U.S. Department of Defense, which suggest that while modern recruits may excel in technical skills, they often fall short in physical and mental toughness compared to previous generations.

The consequences of this unpreparedness can be catastrophic. In combat, hesitation or an inability to cope with stress can lead to loss of life—both for the individual soldier and their comrades. Military training must prepare soldiers for the harshest conditions they may face, and this requires a return to the principles of endurance, resilience, and discipline that once defined boot camp.

RECLAIMING RESILIENCE IN MILITARY TRAINING

To address these challenges, military training must be recalibrated to emphasize physical and mental toughness. Psychological support is important and should be available, but it cannot replace the need for resilience. Training programs should once again push recruits to their limits, ensuring that they are prepared for the extreme conditions of combat. This includes rigorous physical training, exposure to stress, and a renewed focus on unit cohesion, which is critical for success in high-pressure environments.

The military must strike a balance between supporting the mental health of recruits and ensuring that they are exposed to the kind of adversity that will prepare them for the realities of war. Resilience is not built in comfort; it is forged through hardship, challenge, and the confidence that comes from knowing one can endure and overcome adversity.

The softening of military training reflects broader societal shifts, but it comes at the cost of readiness and effectiveness. Combat is brutal and unrelenting, and soldiers must be prepared—both physically and mentally—to face these challenges. The future of military effectiveness depends on a return to the values of resilience, toughness, and endurance. These are the qualities that have always been, and must always remain, at the heart of military service.

UNIVERSITIES: SAFE SPACES AND TRIGGER WARNINGS

Universities have long been heralded as bastions of intellectual challenge and growth, environments where the confrontation of diverse ideas was not only encouraged but expected. These institutions were once the crucibles in which students sharpened their critical thinking skills, learned to engage with opposing viewpoints, and developed the resilience necessary to navigate the complexities of the real world. However, over the past decade, many universities have shifted their focus from intellectual rigor to emotional safety.

This change has introduced concepts like "safe spaces" and "trigger warnings," which aim to protect students from potentially distressing content or ideas, but in doing so, they have altered the educational landscape in ways that raise significant questions about the purpose of higher education.

THE TRADITIONAL ROLE OF UNIVERSITIES: INTELLECTUAL CHALLENGE AND GROWTH

Historically, universities were designed to challenge students intellectually, pushing them to engage with difficult, uncomfortable, and often controversial ideas. The university experience was about exposure to a broad spectrum of perspectives—whether in the sciences, philosophy, politics, or the arts. Students were encouraged to question, debate, and refine their beliefs, often in the face of rigorous opposition from peers and professors alike. The goal was not to coddle students but to prepare them for a world where they would inevitably encounter ideas and situations that would test their values and assumptions.

In these settings, discomfort was seen as an essential part of the learning process. Engaging with opposing viewpoints fostered critical thinking, a skill that universities prized as fundamental to academic and personal development. This was not just about being able to argue effectively; it was about learning to think independently, to sift through evidence, and to build well-reasoned positions that could withstand scrutiny.

The intellectual rigor of this process was challenging by design, as it pushed students to move beyond surface level understanding and engage deeply with the complexities of various subjects.

THE RISE OF SAFE SPACES AND TRIGGER WARNINGS

In recent years, however, the culture at many universities has shifted toward one that prioritizes emotional safety over intellectual challenge. This shift is most evident in the widespread adoption of "safe spaces" and "trigger warnings." A safe space is generally defined as an area—either physical or conceptual—where individuals can retreat from discussions or material that they find uncomfortable or emotionally distressing. Trigger warnings are notices provided before potentially upsetting content, giving students the option to avoid exposure to ideas or images that might cause them psychological discomfort.

The intention behind these measures is rooted in compassion, aiming to accommodate students who may have experienced trauma or who find certain subjects distressing. In practice, however, these policies have led to an environment where intellectual exploration is often curtailed in favor of emotional comfort. Topics such as race, gender, politics, and history—subjects that are inherently complex and sometimes unsettling—are increasingly approached with caution, as professors and students alike navigate a landscape where emotional responses to ideas are given precedence over the rigorous examination of those ideas.

THE BROADER SOCIETAL TREND: AVOIDING DISCOMFORT

The rise of safe spaces and trigger warnings is part of a broader societal trend that places a premium on avoiding discomfort. In many areas of modern life, from education to employment, there is a growing emphasis on shielding individuals from stress, conflict, and emotional strain. While this focus on wellbeing can have positive effects, especially in preventing harm and promoting mental health, it has also led to an unintended consequence: the erosion of emotional resilience.

Emotional resilience—the ability to cope with stress and adapt to challenging situations—is a vital skill, particularly in academic and professional environments. Historically, universities were places where students built this resilience by confronting difficult ideas, enduring criticism, and learning to stand by their convictions in the face of opposition. Today, the emphasis on emotional safety has created a culture where many students are shielded from ideas that might provoke discomfort, leading to concerns that they are ill-prepared to face the complexities of the world outside the university.

THE IMPACT ON INTELLECTUAL FREEDOM AND DEBATE

One of the most significant consequences of the focus on emotional safety is its impact on intellectual freedom and debate. Universities, once proud of fostering environments where all ideas could be freely discussed and debated, are increasingly places where certain topics are avoided, not because they lack academic merit but because they are deemed too controversial or potentially harmful. This has led to self-censorship among students and faculty alike, as the fear of causing offense or being labeled insensitive discourages open dialogue.

The suppression of controversial ideas under the guise of protecting emotional wellbeing has profound implications for the quality of education. Intellectual growth requires exposure to diverse viewpoints, including those that challenge our assumptions. When students are sheltered from controversial or difficult material, they miss the opportunity to grapple with the complexities of these issues and to develop the critical thinking skills necessary to navigate them. Instead of learning to engage with discomfort constructively, students are often encouraged to avoid it altogether.

THE CONSEQUENCES FOR EDUCATION AND SOCIETY

The consequences of this cultural shift extend beyond the university campus. If students are not exposed to intellectual challenges during their time in higher education, they are likely to struggle when they encounter difficult situations in their personal and professional lives. A generation that has been taught to prioritize emotional comfort over resilience may find itself ill-equipped to handle conflict, criticism, and the inherent messiness of real-world decision-making.

Moreover, the decline in robust debate on campuses has broader societal implications. Universities have historically been the breeding grounds for new ideas, the testing grounds for political and social theories, and the incubators of innovation. When these institutions shy away from difficult conversations, society suffers. The absence of rigorous debate stifles intellectual progress and leads to a more fragmented, polarized culture where people are less willing to engage with viewpoints that differ from their own.

RECLAIMING THE UNIVERSITY AS A PLACE OF INTELLECTUAL CHALLENGE

To address these issues, universities must reconsider their role in society and the purpose of higher education. While it is important to support students' mental health and wellbeing, this must not come at the expense of intellectual freedom and the development of resilience. Safe spaces and trigger warnings, if used, should be applied judiciously and in ways that do not undermine the primary goal of education: to challenge students to think critically, engage deeply with complex ideas, and develop the emotional and intellectual fortitude needed to succeed in the world beyond academia.

Universities should once again become environments where discomfort is seen not as something to be avoided but as a necessary part of growth. Students should be encouraged to engage with challenging ideas, to debate openly and respectfully, and to understand that intellectual discomfort is not something to be feared but something to be embraced. Only by confronting difficult ideas can students develop the resilience and critical thinking skills that are essential for success in both their personal and professional lives.

The shift toward safe spaces and trigger warnings reflects a broader societal trend that prioritizes emotional comfort over intellectual challenge. While well-intentioned, this shift risks undermining the very purpose of higher education: to prepare students to engage with the world in all its complexity. To ensure that universities remain places of intellectual growth and exploration, we must reclaim the values of resilience, critical thinking, and open debate. These are the qualities that have always defined higher education and must continue to do so if universities are to fulfill their mission in preparing the next generation for the challenges they will inevitably face.

HISTORICAL COMPARISON: THE GREATEST GENERATION VS. TODAY

To understand the implications of this decline in resilience, it is instructive to compare the experiences of Gen Z with those of the Greatest Generation, those born between 1901 and 1927. The Greatest Generation grew up during the Great Depression and fought in World War II, two of the most challenging periods in modern history. These experiences forged a level of resilience, discipline, and toughness that has become legendary in American cultural memory.

THE GREATEST GENERATION

The Greatest Generation endured profound hardship during the Great Depression, with widespread unemployment and poverty forcing many families to struggle just to survive. Later, during World War II, they were drafted into one of the most brutal conflicts in history, where the stakes were existential, and personal sacrifice was the norm. These individuals faced both physical and emotional adversity, and through these experiences, they developed a remarkable level of resilience and toughness.

This generation's legacy was built on their ability to endure and overcome adversity. After the war, they returned to a society in need of rebuilding. They led the post war economic boom, established stable institutions, and raised families with a strong ethos of discipline, self-sacrifice, and perseverance. Hardship was not something to be avoided; it was seen as an inevitable part of life, one that ultimately strengthened individuals and communities.

Their experiences taught them that resilience is cultivated through facing and overcoming hardship. The Greatest Generation did not have the luxury of avoiding discomfort; instead, they confronted it head on, and this willingness to endure difficult circumstances became a defining characteristic of their identity. The ethos of perseverance and collective responsibility that characterized this generation played a crucial role in shaping the post war era of prosperity and social cohesion.

GEN Z'S PROTECTED ENVIRONMENT

In contrast, Gen Z has grown up in an era of unprecedented convenience, with access to technology, healthcare, and comfort unimaginable to earlier generations. While they face significant global challenges, such as climate change and political instability, their daily lives are often characterized by immediate access to information, entertainment, and services. This convenience, while advantageous in many respects, has also led to a lifestyle where discomfort and hardship are often minimized or entirely avoided.

Universities and even the military, once environments designed to test and toughen individuals, have shifted toward offering greater emotional support and prioritizing comfort over resilience. Many educational institutions focus heavily on creating emotionally supportive environments, which, while important, can sometimes come at the cost of developing the resilience needed to cope with adversity.

While Gen Z is undeniably benefiting from the advancements and sacrifices made by earlier generations, this abundance has also shielded them from the formative experiences that foster resilience. The structures that promote emotional protection, safe spaces, trigger warnings, and other accommodations, are contributing to a culture that is less prepared to handle adversity. Without opportunities to struggle and grow through hardship, younger generations may find themselves lacking the emotional fortitude necessary to navigate life's challenges.

The challenge for Gen Z is not the absence of difficulties but rather the way they are prepared to face them. Encouraging young people to embrace challenges, take risks, and navigate discomfort is crucial for building the resilience that will enable them to thrive in an unpredictable and often harsh world.

THE DECLINE OF PHYSICAL TOUGHNESS

Physical toughness, once a hallmark of resilience, has also declined in recent decades. Physical challenges, whether in military training, sports, or manual labor, have historically played a crucial role in developing mental toughness and self-discipline. Engaging in physically demanding activities teaches individuals to push through discomfort, overcome physical limits, and cultivate the mental strength required to persevere.

Today, however, physical fitness is often viewed as a personal choice rather than a societal expectation, and the emphasis on endurance training has waned. Modern conveniences, such as cars, technology, and desk jobs, have contributed to increasingly sedentary lifestyles. The rise of screen time has further replaced outdoor physical activity, and many young people today are less engaged in activities that test their physical limits.

Statistics on physical activity among young people reflect this decline. According to the U.S. Department of Defense, fewer recruits meet the physical fitness standards required for military service, reflecting broader societal trends where sedentary lifestyles and screen time have replaced physical exertion. This decline in physical toughness has implications beyond health; it weakens the mental toughness and resilience that come from enduring physical challenges.

Sports and physically demanding activities, which once played a significant role in the development of character and resilience, have also seen a decline in participation. Organized sports teach teamwork, discipline, and perseverance, all of which are essential components of resilience. The reduced emphasis on these activities means fewer young people are exposed to the physical and mental challenges that foster toughness and endurance.

To counteract this decline, there must be a renewed focus on encouraging physical activity as a fundamental aspect of education and upbringing. Physical challenges should be embraced as opportunities for growth, teaching young people the value of perseverance, discipline, and the satisfaction of pushing beyond their limits.

REBUILDING RESILIENCE: A PATH FORWARD

The shift from resilience to emotional protection has defined much of the modern experience for younger generations, whether in the military, educational institutions, or broader societal norms. While mental health and emotional well-being are critical, overprotection risks fostering a generation unprepared to handle life's inevitable hardships. The challenge is to strike a balance between providing support and fostering resilience, ensuring that young people are equipped to handle the complexities of adulthood.

The experiences of the Greatest Generation offer a valuable lesson in the benefits of enduring and overcoming adversity. While it is neither desirable nor practical to recreate the extreme conditions they faced, it is essential to strike a balance between empathy and resilience building. This means encouraging young people to face discomfort, challenge themselves physically and mentally, and engage with opposing viewpoints rather than avoiding them.

Resilience is not built by sheltering individuals from hardship but by equipping them to endure and grow from challenges. By fostering an environment where discomfort is embraced as part of growth, society can help cultivate a generation ready to meet the world's challenges head on, armed with resilience, fortitude, and a belief in their own capacity to endure and thrive.

REBUILDING A CULTURE OF RESILIENCE

The growing fragility seen in educational institutions, workplaces, and even within military ranks is a reflection of a broader societal trend that prioritizes emotional comfort over resilience. This shift has resulted in a generation that is often ill-equipped to handle life's complexities, lacking the mental toughness, emotional resilience, and intellectual rigor needed to confront challenges. To reverse this trend, society must actively work to rebuild these values across various institutions. This requires a fundamental recalibration of how we approach education, physical fitness, and emotional wellbeing, moving away from overprotection and toward fostering the grit necessary to thrive in an increasingly complex world.

THE EROSION OF RESILIENCE: A SOCIETAL PROBLEM

In recent years, there has been a noticeable erosion of resilience across many sectors of society. Emotional resilience—the ability to recover from setbacks, cope with stress, and adapt to adversity—has been undermined by a culture that increasingly seeks to shield individuals from discomfort. In education, workplaces, and public discourse, there is a growing tendency to avoid conflict, minimize stress, and prioritize emotional safety over growth.

This cultural shift has not come without consequences. By prioritizing comfort, society has inadvertently stunted the development of crucial skills needed to navigate a world that is, by nature, unpredictable and often unforgiving. When individuals are not given the opportunity to face challenges head-on, they are deprived of the chance to develop the mental toughness and problem-solving abilities that come from enduring difficulty.

THE NEED FOR RECALIBRATION IN EDUCATION

Education plays a critical role in shaping the values and capabilities of future generations. However, the shift toward emotional protection in schools and universities has created environments where intellectual rigor is often sacrificed for the sake of emotional comfort. Safe spaces and trigger warnings, while rooted in a desire to protect students from distress, can lead to an educational experience that lacks the depth and challenge necessary for intellectual growth.

To rebuild resilience, educational institutions must once again prioritize critical thinking and intellectual rigor. Students must be exposed to a wide range of ideas, including those that challenge their beliefs or cause discomfort. This exposure is essential for developing the ability to engage with complex issues, think independently, and build the resilience needed to navigate a world filled with uncertainty and conflicting viewpoints.

In practice, this means encouraging open debate and discussion in classrooms, even on controversial or difficult topics. It means fostering an environment where students learn to engage with opposing perspectives thoughtfully and respectfully, without retreating into intellectual or emotional safe zones. By embracing discomfort as part of the learning process, students can develop the intellectual resilience necessary to face the complexities of the real world.

PHYSICAL FITNESS: BUILDING TOUGHNESS IN BODY AND MIND

Physical fitness is another area where society must recalibrate its approach to foster resilience. The decline in physical fitness, particularly among younger generations, reflects a broader disengagement from the values of discipline, endurance, and toughness. Rising rates of obesity and sedentary lifestyles, coupled with the diminishing emphasis on physical education in schools, have contributed to a generation that is less physically prepared for the demands of life.

However, physical fitness is not just about health, it is closely linked to mental toughness. Physical exertion, whether through sports, exercise, or physical labor, teaches individuals to push through discomfort, set goals, and persevere in the face of challenges. These qualities translate directly into mental resilience, as the experience of overcoming physical barriers builds the confidence to tackle other forms of adversity.

To address this, schools, workplaces, and communities must reemphasize the importance of physical fitness. This can be done by reintegrating rigorous physical education programs into school curriculums, promoting sports and physical challenges, and encouraging individuals to engage in regular physical activity. By fostering both physical and mental toughness through physical fitness, society can equip individuals with the resilience needed to face life's inevitable challenges.

EMOTIONAL WELLBEING: RESILIENCE OVER COMFORT

While emotional wellbeing is a legitimate concern, the current cultural focus on avoiding stress and discomfort has gone too far in promoting fragility. Emotional wellbeing should not be equated with emotional avoidance. True emotional resilience is not built by sheltering individuals from stress but by teaching them how to manage it effectively. Coping with adversity is a crucial life skill that can only be developed through exposure to difficult situations, not by being shielded from them.

To recalibrate our approach to emotional wellbeing, we must shift the focus from overprotection to resilience building. This means teaching individuals, from a young age, how to cope with stress, manage their emotions, and recover from setbacks. Schools can incorporate resilience training into their curriculums, helping students develop the emotional tools they need to handle challenges without becoming overwhelmed. In the workplace, resilience programs can help employees manage stress more effectively, fostering an environment where individuals are better equipped to navigate the demands of their jobs without burnout.

EMBRACING GRIT: A PATH FORWARD

The cultivation of resilience, mental toughness, and intellectual rigor requires a societal embrace of grit—the ability to persevere in the face of difficulty and maintain focus on long-term goals. Grit is not just a personal trait; it is a value that society must nurture across all institutions. In schools, grit is fostered by challenging students academically, encouraging perseverance, and rewarding effort over immediate success. In the workplace, grit is encouraged by setting high expectations, promoting a culture of accountability, and valuing persistence in the face of obstacles.

Ultimately, rebuilding resilience requires a collective effort to recalibrate how we approach discomfort and challenge. By embracing grit as a foundational value, we can foster a culture that prizes resilience over fragility, toughness over avoidance, and growth over comfort.

REBUILDING FOR THE FUTURE

Addressing the growing fragility in society requires a fundamental shift in how we think about resilience, toughness, and intellectual rigor. In education, we must return to the principles of intellectual challenge and open debate, rejecting the overprotective measures that stifle growth. In physical fitness, we must reemphasize the importance of endurance, discipline, and physical toughness as essential components of overall wellbeing. And in emotional health, we must teach resilience, helping individuals learn to navigate stress and discomfort rather than avoiding it.

By making these changes, we can rebuild a society that values and cultivates the grit necessary to face life's complexities with strength and determination. Resilience is not a luxury—it is a necessity for navigating the challenges of the modern world. If we are to thrive as individuals and as a society, we must reclaim the values that foster toughness, perseverance, and growth in the face of adversity. Only by embracing discomfort as an integral part of life can we hope to build a future that is stronger, more resilient, and better equipped to handle the inevitable challenges ahead.

REJECTING THE SNOWFLAKE MENTALITY: A CALL FOR ACCOUNTABILITY

We've made life too easy, and in doing so, we've not just allowed but created a generation of "snowflakes." This mentality has permeated society, fostering entitlement, fragility, and self-importance. We've let the snowflake ideology take hold, where people believe their every feeling— no matter how fleeting or trivial—demands acknowledgment and validation. This is a mindset we must confront head-on.

It's time to say: you are not that special. Not every thought in your head needs to be voiced. You are not above the rules or the law. No one cares who your father is, and the police are not your "bro." The world is not here to accommodate your discomfort or protect you from life's realities. Most snowflakes don't need counseling; they need a healthy dose of reality. The fact is society is tired of carrying you. You are dead weight.

So, suck it up, snowflake. Suck it up or melt. Get on board or wither away into nothingness. Perhaps, in the end, you'll serve as a good reminder of what not to be. Either way, it's time to reclaim a culture that values resilience over fragility, accountability over entitlement, and toughness over self-indulgence. The sooner we reject this snowflake mentality, the stronger, more capable, and more grounded our society will become.

CHAPTER SIX

GENDER CONFUSION

The rapid cultural transformation in modern gender dynamics has created a generation increasingly untethered from the traditional values that provided societal stability for decades. The feminization of men and the masculinization of women has disrupted established norms, leading to widespread confusion about identity, roles, and relationships. This shift has had tangible effects on personal dynamics, professional interactions, and family stability, ultimately weakening the social fabric that once bound communities together.

At the heart of this transformation lies a fundamental misunderstanding of the value inherent in both traditional masculinity and femininity. Assertive male behaviors are now labeled as "toxic masculinity," while women are pressured to embody traditionally masculine traits like aggressiveness and competitiveness to succeed in male dominated spheres. The result is a cultural milieu where both men and women are losing their sense of identity, leaving them dissatisfied, disconnected, and increasingly unsure of their place in the world. Rising divorce rates, mounting discontent in relationships, and a palpable crisis of identity among both genders are clear signs of this imbalance.

INFLUENCE OF LIBERAL IDEOLOGY AND LGBTQ+ ACTIVISM

The feminization of men and the masculinization of women are not organic cultural shift but is often actively promoted by liberal ideologies, particularly those tied to modern progressive movements and LGBTQ+ activism. The growing push for gender fluidity, nonbinary identities, and the dismantling of traditional gender roles is rooted in liberal and socialist frameworks that seek to deconstruct historical social structures. Many of these movements—while advocating for equality and inclusion—have contributed to a broader confusion about what it means to be male or female, and what roles individuals should occupy in society.

Many LGBTQ+ activists, as well as liberal democrats, champion the idea that traditional masculinity and femininity are restrictive, outdated constructs. Instead, they promote gender as a spectrum, encouraging individuals to reject binary notions of male and female. While the aim of these movements is to foster greater inclusivity and acceptance of nontraditional gender identities, they have also contributed to a broader cultural shift that undermines the value of traditionally masculine and feminine traits. This push often discourages men from embracing their natural assertiveness or competitiveness, and pressures women to adopt traits like aggression and independence to be successful.

Liberal ideologies, especially those influenced by socialist thought, support the idea that gender roles should be fluid and interchangeable, promoting policies that prioritize the dismantling of gender norms. This is evident in educational curriculums that emphasize gender neutrality and in media portrayals that celebrate nontraditional gender expressions. While these efforts should challenge stereotypes and promote equality, they often have the unintended consequence of blurring the lines between masculinity and femininity, leading to confusion in personal identity and societal roles.

THE FEMINIZATION OF MEN

In recent decades, traditionally masculine traits—assertiveness, stoicism, competitiveness, and physical strength—have come under increasing cultural scrutiny. What began as an effort to address harmful behaviors associated with "toxic masculinity," such as unchecked aggression or emotional repression, has gradually morphed into a broader attack on masculinity itself. Today, even positive masculine qualities like leadership, courage, and resilience are frequently questioned, if not outright vilified.

This cultural demonization has contributed to a crisis in male identity. Young men are increasingly pressured to reject traditionally masculine traits in favor of more socially acceptable qualities such as heightened sensitivity and passivity. Boys grow up hearing that their natural tendencies toward assertiveness and competitiveness are problematic, leading to confusion and a diminished sense of self-worth. This uncertainty leaves many young men without a clear sense of purpose or direction, eroding their confidence and undermining their potential.

The effects are widespread. Male enrollment in higher education has dropped significantly, and men now make up a much smaller proportion of college students than previous generations. Many young men are disengaging from the pursuit of traditional success markers—stable employment, long-term relationships, and family life—choosing instead to retreat into escapism through video games, social media, and other distractions that offer temporary refuge from societal pressures. The rise of terms like "failure to launch" and the growing prevalence of "incel" culture only further illustrate the deepening male identity crisis.

POPULAR MEDIA AND MALE ROLE MODELS

Popular media plays a significant role in shaping cultural perceptions of masculinity. In today's films and television, men are often portrayed as either emotionally clueless buffoons or hyperaggressive, toxic figures. These one-dimensional depictions leave young men with few positive role models to emulate. Healthy masculinity, where strength is balanced with empathy—has become increasingly rare in media portrayals. Without relatable examples of positive masculinity, young men are left adrift, unsure of how to channel their natural strengths productively.

Liberal driven media often reinforces these problematic portrayals, pushing the narrative that traditional male behaviors are outdated or harmful. Instead of showing men as strong, assertive, and responsible, many shows and movies emphasize weakness, passivity, or emasculation as the new norm. This shift leaves young men confused about what is expected of them, contributing to their disconnection from both traditional values and contemporary expectations.

RECLAIMING HEALTHY MASCULINITY

The path forward for men is not to deny or suppress their masculine traits but to reframe them in a positive and constructive light. Assertiveness, competitiveness, and stoicism—when harnessed appropriately—can be powerful forces for personal and societal good. Programs aimed at mentoring boys and young men can play a critical role in this effort. Community mentorship initiatives that connect experienced men with young boys offer valuable examples of how masculinity can embody strength, honor, empathy, and integrity.

Educational systems must recognize and accommodate the unique needs of boys. Providing outlets for physical energy and opportunities for leadership is crucial to helping young men develop their identities without feeling stigmatized for their natural inclinations. By embracing a more balanced view of masculinity, society can cultivate men who are both strong and compassionate, competitive, yet empathetic.

THE MASCULINIZATION OF WOMEN

On the other end of the spectrum, society has increasingly encouraged women to adopt traits traditionally associated with masculinity—assertiveness, competitiveness, and independence—to succeed in professional environments. While the push for gender equality is critical, it has often translated into an expectation that women must conform to traditionally male standards of success in order to be valued. This has created a growing disconnect between women and their authentic selves.

This trend is often reinforced by liberal ideologies, which emphasize that women must "lean in" to male dominated spheres in order to be considered equal. The underlying message is that traditionally feminine traits—nurturing, empathy, and cooperation—are secondary to the masculine traits of ambition and competitiveness. As a result, many women feel pressured to suppress their natural inclinations and adopt behaviors that are not in line with their true identities.

CORPORATE PRESSURES AND GENDER EXPECTATIONS

Nowhere is this pressure more evident than in the corporate world, where women are often expected to exhibit the same levels of drive and ambition as their male counterparts—sometimes at the expense of their wellbeing. Women who choose to prioritize family or embrace traditionally feminine traits like nurturing are often stigmatized as less committed to their careers. Meanwhile, the societal expectation that women must succeed in both the workplace and the home leaves many feeling overwhelmed and unfulfilled.

This shift has had tangible consequences. Declining birth rates, delayed family planning, and rising levels of anxiety and depression among women are all indicators of the toll this relentless pressure is taking. Women increasingly feel as though they must "do it all"—climb the corporate ladder, maintain a perfect household, and nurture relationships—while suppressing their natural inclinations toward empathy and cooperation.

A BALANCED APPROACH TO EMPOWERMENT

The solution is not to discourage women from pursuing ambitious goals, but to recognize and celebrate the diverse strengths they bring to the table. Traits traditionally associated with femininity—empathy, cooperation, and nurturing—are just as valuable as those associated with masculinity. We must foster a society that allows women to thrive in whatever roles they choose, without imposing the expectation that they must sacrifice their authentic selves to succeed.

Companies should implement policies that promote flexibility and work-life balance, enabling women (and men) to pursue their professional aspirations without sacrificing personal wellbeing. Additionally, media representations of women that highlight both strength and compassion are crucial in reshaping societal norms and expectations.

CONFUSION IN DATING AND WORKPLACE DYNAMICS

The evolving gender roles have also introduced significant confusion in both dating and workplace dynamics. In dating, traditional norms that once guided courtship have been upended, leading to uncertainty about what men and women expect from each other. Men are often hesitant to take initiative for fear of being labeled too aggressive, while women may feel frustrated when expected to take on more traditionally masculine roles in romantic pursuits. This role reversal frequently leaves both parties dissatisfied, as they find themselves acting against their instincts.

Similarly, in the workplace, women are expected to assert themselves to succeed, while men may feel pressured to step back to avoid appearing domineering. These conflicting expectations create an imbalance, making collaboration and communication more difficult as individuals struggle to navigate new, often unspoken, rules.

CULTIVATING CLARITY AND AUTHENTICITY

To address these challenges, we must promote a culture of authenticity, where both men and women are encouraged to embrace their natural strengths and communicate openly. In the workplace, this means fostering environments that value diverse leadership styles and allow individuals to take on roles that align with their strengths. Leaders should encourage a balance of empathy and assertiveness, recognizing that both are necessary for a healthy and productive environment.

In relationships, individuals must feel empowered to express their desires and expectations without fear of judgment or stigma. Open communication about gender roles, values, and expectations can help alleviate much of the confusion surrounding modern dating and professional dynamics.

By fostering open dialogue, we can break down the barriers that currently create confusion and frustration in relationships and workplaces alike. The emphasis should be on authenticity, where both men and women are free to express their desires, ambitions, and natural traits without fear of judgment or societal backlash. Relationships, whether romantic or professional, thrive when individuals are allowed to be their true selves, rather than conforming to externally imposed expectations.

THE IMPACT ON FAMILY AND SOCIETY: EROSION OF STABILITY

The shifts in gender roles promoted by liberal ideologies and reinforced through media, academia, and popular culture have also had profound effects on family structures and societal stability. Historically, traditional gender roles provided a clear framework within which families operated. Though not without flaws, these roles offered predictability and stability that supported family wellbeing. Men and women each had defined responsibilities that complemented each other, creating a cohesive unit.

As these traditional roles have become increasingly blurred, many families are struggling to find a balance that works for them. The pressure for both partners to excel professionally while managing household responsibilities has led to rising tension and instability in families. With both men and women expected to embody conflicting traits, they often feel overwhelmed by the demands of modern life.

Parents who are overburdened with career pressures may find it difficult to engage meaningfully with their children. This decline in quality time spent with family members erodes the emotional bonds that once provided security and stability. As both men and women navigate the competing demands of career, family, and personal identity, the lack of clearly defined roles within the household leads to disarray and confusion. The traditional family unit, which once served as a pillar of societal stability, is increasingly at risk.

CONSEQUENCES: RISING DIVORCE AND DECLINING BIRTH RATES

The consequences of these shifting dynamics are apparent in the statistics. Divorce rates continue to rise, birth rates are declining, and more couples are choosing to delay or forgo family planning altogether. These trends reflect not just individual decisions but a broader societal shift away from the traditional values that once emphasized family as a central, stabilizing force.

Children, too, are affected by this cultural shift. Growing up in environments where parental roles are unclear and family stability is weakened, many children struggle with their own sense of identity and purpose. Without strong family structures to guide them, they are more likely to face difficulties in school, social settings, and later in life. The long-term effects of this instability are far-reaching, contributing to the broader sense of societal decline.

REIMAGINING FAMILY ROLES FOR STABILITY

To rebuild stable family structures, society must embrace flexible yet defined roles that allow both men and women to contribute in meaningful ways. This means rejecting the idea that one gender must suppress its natural traits to succeed, while the other is forced to adopt unfamiliar behaviors. Fathers should be encouraged to take on nurturing roles without fear of being stigmatized, and mothers should be supported in their professional ambitions without being seen as neglectful of family duties.

Public policies that promote work-life balance, such as paid parental leave and flexible working hours, can play a crucial role in creating a culture that values both family wellbeing and professional success. Encouraging family centered community activities and fostering strong support networks for parents can help restore the sense of connection and belonging that has been lost in modern society.

ROLE OF MEDIA AND EDUCATION

Media and educational institutions have a significant role to play in reshaping how we think about gender roles and family dynamics. Unfortunately, in recent years, many have taken this role as a mandate to promote a confusing array of ideologies that prioritize certain narratives over common sense and balance. Rather than pushing narratives that force men and women into rigid molds or dismantle traditional values altogether, the media and education should promote a balanced approach that celebrates the unique contributions of both genders. Positive representations of both masculinity and femininity—where men can be strong and empathetic, and women can be assertive and nurturing—will help future generations understand that strength and compassion are not mutually exclusive. A balanced portrayal like this will enable individuals to take pride in their strengths while understanding the value of others' differences.

Schools and universities, too, must reconsider how they approach gender education. Increasingly, activist teachers who are themselves confused about gender are taking it upon themselves to push agendas in classrooms that are more about activism than education. With pride flags, BLM banners, and other symbols of ideological activism adorning classrooms, public education is being overtaken by specific political viewpoints that promote a one-sided understanding of gender and social justice issues. This environment puts children at risk of feeling overwhelmed, confused, and pressured into adopting beliefs about themselves that may not align with their personal experiences or developing identities. Educators should not be in the business of identity re-engineering but rather fostering a balanced exploration of gender dynamics that respects traditional values as well as contemporary discussions.

Instead of promoting extreme forms of gender fluidity or dismantling traditional roles entirely, educators should focus on helping students understand the strengths inherent in both masculine and feminine characteristics. By teaching students the value of both masculine and feminine traits, young people can learn how to navigate their own identities without feeling pressured to conform to any particular ideological agenda. It is important that education returns to encouraging critical thinking and diverse perspectives rather than an unquestioned acceptance of the latest social trends. The classroom should be a space where students learn how to analyze, question, and understand complex societal dynamics, including gender, in a manner that respects both the traditions that many still hold dear and the evolving landscape of social identity.

Media also plays a pivotal role in shaping societal norms and values. The current trend of sensationalism and identity-driven narratives often feeds into a culture that perpetuates division rather than fosters understanding. Media coverage that encourages narrow portrayals of masculinity as inherently toxic or femininity as oppressive only furthers this divide. The solution lies in a more nuanced portrayal—where boys and men are seen as capable of empathy, and girls and women are recognized for their resilience and leadership. By presenting balanced narratives, the media can encourage a culture where strength and sensitivity coexist, and where gender identity is not used as a divisive tool.

Ultimately, it is crucial that both media and education resist the temptation to force ideologies on impressionable minds. Our children deserve to grow up in an environment where they are taught to think for themselves, respect others' beliefs, and navigate their own path. There is no place for activism that seeks to dismantle the core values of family, community, and self-understanding. The aim should be to inspire individuals to celebrate both their unique identities and their shared humanity—without coercion, confusion, or the intrusion of political agendas that belong outside of the classroom and beyond the influence of mass media. The role of these institutions should be to uplift, inform, and empower—not to shape individuals according to a preconceived social script that may or may not stand the test of time.

REBALANCING GENDER ROLES FOR A STABLE SOCIETY

The solution to the confusion and dissatisfaction caused by the feminization of men and the masculinization of women is not to revert to outdated and rigid gender roles, but to recognize the inherent value in both masculine and feminine traits. Society thrives when men are encouraged to be both strong and compassionate, and when women are empowered to be both assertive and nurturing.

True equality is not achieved by forcing men and women to abandon their natural inclinations in favor of societal expectations. Instead, it comes from creating an environment where both genders feel valued for their unique strengths and are given the freedom to contribute meaningfully to society in ways that align with their identities.

By fostering a cultural shift that honors the strengths of both masculinity and femininity, we can create a more stable and balanced society. Encouraging men to embrace assertiveness without fear of societal backlash and allowing women the freedom to embody both traditionally masculine and feminine traits, will lead to a world where individuals are not confined by ideology but are empowered to be their true selves. In this way, we can reverse the trend of societal confusion, restore stability in families, and build a society where strength and empathy, leadership and compassion, coexist in harmony.

RESTORING BALANCE

The feminization of men and the masculinization of women, driven by liberal ideologies and reinforced by media and educational institutions, have disrupted the natural order of gender roles, leading to confusion and dissatisfaction across relationships, workplaces, and families. However, with deliberate action, we can recalibrate these shifts, honoring the strengths of both masculinity and femininity to create a society that is stable, strong, and united.

The path forward lies in embracing both tradition and progress—understanding that true equality means respecting the differences that make us unique, rather than forcing a homogenization of roles that ultimately serves no one. By reclaiming the positive aspects of masculinity and femininity, we can restore a sense of purpose, direction, and fulfillment in individuals and society.

CHAPTER SEVEN

PROLONGED ADOLESCENCE

Traditionally, leaving home was a rite of passage that marked the transition from adolescence to adulthood. For generations, young adults moved out in their early twenties, seeking to establish their own households, careers, and families. However, today's norm has shifted. Data from the Pew Research Center reveals that over 50% of young adults aged 18 to 29 were living with their parents in 2020, reaching levels not seen since the Great Depression. Economic pressures such as high student loan debt, rising housing costs, and a volatile job market are frequently cited as the reasons for this shift. But while finances play a role, they do not tell the full story.

The reality is that many young adults remain at home not because they cannot afford to move out but because they find it easier — and more comfortable — to stay. With rent-free living, food provided, and utilities covered, there is little incentive for them to leave the nest. This arrangement may seem harmless on the surface, but it ultimately fosters a culture of dependency that undermines the development of self-sufficiency and personal responsibility. However, the fault does not rest solely on Generation Z; their parents are equally to blame for enabling this prolonged adolescence.

THE ROLE OF PARENTS: ENABLING DEPENDENCY

Parents today often fail to recognize that their well-intentioned efforts to protect and support their children can have unintended consequences. By allowing adult children to live at home without contributing to household expenses—whether it be rent, utilities, or groceries—parents create an environment where young adults are shielded from the realities of adulthood. In previous generations, parents pushed their children to leave home and stand on their own two feet, understanding that independence was necessary for personal growth. But in today's world, many parents seem content to continue providing for their children well into adulthood, fostering a sense of entitlement and dependence.

This is not just a Gen Z problem; it is a failure of parenting. Parents, particularly those who came of age during the Baby Boomer era or Generation X, grew up in environments where independence was expected. Yet, they have become increasingly reluctant to hold their own children to the same standards. Many are overly protective, unwilling to let their children experience hardship, make mistakes, or face financial pressures. This reluctance to let go perpetuates a cycle of dependency, where young adults are deprived of the opportunity to learn essential life skills such as budgeting, problem-solving, and decision-making. By providing a financial and emotional safety net long after it is necessary, parents are stifling their children's development.

THE SYMBOLISM OF LUGGAGE: A PUSH FOR INDEPENDENCE

One of the most valuable gifts a parent can give their 18yearold is not more time at home but a piece of luggage. The act of giving luggage is symbolic—a clear message that it is time to leave the nest and begin the journey into adulthood. Encouraging young adults to move out, take on responsibilities, and navigate life's challenges is essential for their growth. Yet too often, parents do the opposite. Instead of fostering independence, they enable prolonged adolescence by allowing their children to remain at home rent-free, contributing nothing toward household expenses or maintenance.

This approach denies young adults the invaluable experience of managing their own lives. The harsh reality is that independence cannot be achieved without struggle. When parents provide everything for their adult children—shelter, food, insurance—they remove any real incentive for these young adults to develop self-reliance. This dynamic creates a demented system of dependency that robs young people of the personal growth that comes from facing challenges, overcoming difficulties, and ultimately learning to fend for themselves.

DELAYED LIFE MILESTONES: A CULTURAL SHIFT

For generations, milestones such as leaving home, getting married, buying a house, and starting a career were considered markers of adulthood. Today, these milestones are delayed or abandoned altogether. Homeownership rates among young adults have significantly decreased, with many choosing to rent indefinitely or live with their parents. According to data from Zillow, the average age of first-time homeownership continues to rise, as young adults increasingly prioritize flexibility over stability. Likewise, marriage rates have plummeted, with many young adults delaying marriage or choosing not to marry at all. Gallup data reveals that fewer Gen Z adults are getting married than any previous generation, preferring instead to focus on personal development and career exploration.

However, it is not just financial barriers that are delaying these life milestones. The comfort and security provided by living at home play a significant role. When young adults can rely on their parents for financial and emotional support, there is little urgency to pursue the traditional markers of adulthood.

Why rush into a mortgage or marriage when life at home offers comfort without consequence?

PARENTS' ROLE IN DELAYING INDEPENDENCE

Parents, you are complicit in creating a generation ill-equipped to face the real world. By failing to set boundaries and enforce expectations, you've allowed your adult children to linger in a state of extended adolescence, all while telling yourselves you're "helping them figure things out." Let's be honest—you're not helping; you're hindering. Every time you offer a financial bailout or a cushy return to the family home, you prevent them from facing the very challenges that build resilience and character.

It's your responsibility to stop coddling and start pushing your children toward independence. Instead of allowing them to coast on your dime, demand they contribute. Make them pay rent, cover their own bills, and take on responsibilities that will prepare them for life outside your household. The world isn't going to hand them a free pass, and neither should you. By enforcing these realities now, you'll teach them financial discipline, work ethic, and self-reliance—the qualities they need to survive on their own.

Stop making excuses for them. The longer you delay their independence, the longer they'll remain dependent, weak, and unprepared for life's demands. You aren't doing them any favors by being their safety net. If you truly want to help your children, cut the cord, set expectations, and make them earn their way. It's time to stop enabling and start preparing them for the real world—because it won't wait forever.

HISTORICAL PARALLELS: COMFORT AND THE DECLINE OF EMPIRES

The modern trend of prolonged adolescence and dependence on parental support mirrors the patterns seen in declining empires throughout history. Sir John Glubb's famous essay The Fate of Empires outlines the stages of an empire's lifecycle, noting that in the final phases, societies become consumed with luxury and comfort, abandoning the hard work and discipline that originally led to their rise. In these societies, citizens become increasingly dependent on others for their wellbeing, avoiding the struggles necessary to sustain growth and innovation.

The Roman Empire provides a striking example. At its height, Roman citizens were known for their discipline, military prowess, and dedication to civic duty. But as Rome grew wealthy and comfortable, its citizens became dependent on luxuries and conveniences, avoiding the hardships that once made the empire great. This retreat into comfort and dependency contributed to Rome's decline, leaving it vulnerable to external threats and internal collapse.

In much the same way, today's young adults, with the enabling support of their parents, are retreating into comfort and avoiding the responsibilities that come with adulthood. When individuals fail to take on challenges and contribute to society, the collective strength of that society weakens. The parallels between Generation Z's prolonged adolescence and the decline of past empires should serve as a warning.

THE PSYCHOLOGICAL IMPACT OF COMFORT

Staying at home may offer young adults immediate financial and emotional comfort, but it comes at a significant cost. By postponing the responsibilities of independent living, they miss out on the life experiences that build resilience and character. The challenges of managing bills, maintaining a home, and navigating personal conflicts are essential to personal growth.

LACK OF RESILIENCE

Numerous psychological studies show that young adults who delay moving out and facing life's challenges are less likely to develop resilience. Without the pressure of paying rent, managing a budget, or handling conflicts independently, they are shielded from the stressors that cultivate emotional maturity. When parents provide for their adult children in every aspect of life, they rob them of the opportunity to build the problem-solving skills necessary for success.

THE COMFORT TRAP

The longer young adults remain in their comfort zones, the harder it becomes to leave. The more comfortable life at home becomes, the less motivated they are to seek independence. Psychologists warn that comfort, when allowed to dominate, leads to complacency. In today's society, where comfort is readily available, young adults are less inclined to step outside their comfort zones to pursue the independence and resilience that adulthood requires.

BREAKING THE CYCLE OF DEPENDENCY

The solution to this cultural malaise lies in shifting the attitudes of both parents and young adults. For parents, it means setting boundaries and refusing to subsidize prolonged adolescence. Giving your adult child a piece of luggage, rather than endless financial support, is a critical step toward encouraging independence. For young adults, it means recognizing that personal growth requires stepping into discomfort—facing challenges, making mistakes, and learning to stand on one's own.

Breaking free from the cycle of dependency will require a cultural recalibration that reestablishes independence, responsibility, and resilience as the cornerstones of adulthood. Parents must take an active role in pushing their children toward these values, rather than enabling complacency. Only by doing so can we create a society of strong, capable individuals who are prepared to contribute meaningfully to the world around them.

RESTORING INDEPENDENCE

The prolonged adolescence of Generation Z is not just a symptom of economic hardship—it is the result of a broader cultural shift where parents and young adults alike have prioritized comfort over growth. Staying at home may seem like the easier choice, but it ultimately stunts personal development and weakens society. Parents, by enabling this dependency, bear a significant share of the responsibility.

To reverse this trend, we must reemphasize the importance of independence, self-sufficiency, and resilience. Young adults need to face life's challenges, and parents need to give them the push to do so. Independence is not a punishment—it is a gift, one that fosters the confidence and skills necessary for a fulfilling life. Only by breaking free from the comfort of home can young adults truly grow into capable, contributing members of society.

CHAPTER EIGHT

Ineffective Parenting

The emergence of Generation Z parents, themselves shaped by permissiveness, instant gratification, and societal coddling, now threatens to deepen the generational decline already in motion. With parenting styles that oscillate between helicopter level over-involvement and lax permissiveness, these parents are raising children who are even more disconnected from the principles of discipline, responsibility, and self-sufficiency. This chapter examines how the failure to set boundaries, enforce consistent discipline, and embrace the discomfort of parenting has resulted in children running the household—leaving them woefully unprepared for the challenges of adult life and accelerating societal decay.

HELICOPTER PARENTING EVOLVING INTO PERMISSIVE PARENTING

In recent decades, helicopter parenting—characterized by constant oversight, excessive involvement, and an obsessive need to protect children from failure—dominated the landscape of modern parenting. Many Millennial and Gen X parents embraced this method out of a desire to shield their children from the harshness of life. However, Generation Z parents have taken this protective instinct one step further, evolving it into a permissive parenting style that is even more damaging. Rather than merely overseeing their children's lives, Gen Z parents are granting near total autonomy, abdicating their role as authority figures and instead allowing their children to dictate the terms of their upbringing.

FROM OVERINVOLVEMENT TO LACK OF BOUNDARIES

While helicopter parenting involved constant intervention, permissive parenting takes the opposite approach—offering children almost complete freedom with few boundaries. Many Gen Z parents, raised in an era where personal comfort and emotional validation were paramount, are hesitant to impose rules or discipline. This hesitancy stems from the fear of upsetting their children, or worse, not being liked by them. The desire to be seen as a friend rather than an authority figure has given rise to a generation of children who lack structure and discipline, leaving them ill-equipped for the realities of the world.

A report by the American Academy of Pediatrics highlights the dangers of permissive parenting. Children raised in these environments struggle with self-discipline, have difficulty regulating their emotions, and are often unable to respect authority figures. Without clear expectations or consequences, children come to expect that their desires will always be prioritized, reinforcing a sense of entitlement. These early lessons create lifelong patterns of behavior, where individuals believe they deserve rewards without the corresponding effort.

CHILDREN RUNNING THE HOUSEHOLD

One of the most glaring consequences of permissive parenting is the shift in power dynamics within the home. Many households today are effectively run by the children, with parents ceding authority to avoid conflict. Whether it's indulging unreasonable demands or refusing to enforce rules, many Gen Z parents find themselves at the mercy of their children's whims. The traditional hierarchy, where parents set the rules and children are expected to follow them, has been eroded, leading to a chaotic family structure.

Psychologist Dr. Leonard Sax, in his book The Collapse of Parenting, warns of the dangers of this inversion of roles. He argues that when parents treat children as equals in decision-making, without regard for their maturity or experience, they send a message that authority and rules are optional. This leaves children ill-prepared to function in environments that require respect for hierarchy and authority, such as schools, workplaces, and social institutions. Children who grow up running the household often struggle to adapt to structured settings, where their opinions and desires do not always take precedence.

BEHAVIORAL ISSUES ARISING FROM LACK OF DISCIPLINE

Permissive parenting inevitably leads to behavioral problems. Without a framework of discipline or clearly defined rules, children do not learn to respect authority or understand the concept of consequences. This permissive environment fosters impulsive, aggressive, and socially disruptive behavior, as children come to believe that their actions have no limits or repercussions.

LACK OF STRUCTURE LEADS TO BEHAVIORAL PROBLEMS

Research published in the Journal of Child Development reveals that children raised in homes without clear boundaries are far more likely to exhibit behavioral issues, including defiance, impulsivity, and aggression. Without consistent discipline, children are left to their own devices, often pushing the limits of acceptable behavior. This lack of structure creates confusion about right and wrong, leading to poor social interactions and difficulty in adhering to rules in more formal environments like schools.

Educational institutions are increasingly reporting issues with students who are unable to follow instructions or accept authority. Teachers find that many students raised in permissive households are resistant to correction, unable to resolve conflicts, and prone to emotional outbursts when they don't get their way. This not only disrupts learning but also places an additional burden on educators to teach basic life skills that should have been instilled at home.

EMOTIONAL FRAGILITY AND ENTITLEMENT

Children raised without boundaries are not only prone to behavioral issues but also develop a heightened sense of entitlement. By rarely facing the consequences of their actions or learning the value of hard work, these children come to expect that their needs and desires will always be met. When reality inevitably fails to meet these expectations, emotional fragility sets in, as they are unable to cope with setbacks, failure, or rejection.

FRAGILE MINDS, FRAGILE EMOTIONS

A study conducted by Stanford University highlights the link between permissive parenting and increased rates of anxiety and depression among children. When children are shielded from adversity, they miss out on the opportunity to build resilience and coping mechanisms. As a result, they are more likely to suffer from mental health issues when faced with even the most routine challenges of life. A generation raised to believe that their emotional comfort is paramount struggles to handle disappointment or criticism.

These children grow into adults who cannot function in environments that demand perseverance, responsibility, or emotional regulation. The rise of entitlement culture, where individuals believe they are owed success, rewards, or validation without putting in the work, can be traced back to this lack of discipline in early childhood. This emotional fragility is not only damaging to the individual but also to the society that must accommodate it.

THE IMPACT ON SOCIETY: RAISING A GENERATION OF ENTITLEMENT

The societal costs of permissive parenting extend far beyond individual households. By raising children without discipline, structure, or accountability, Gen Z parents are fostering a generation that is even more disconnected from the responsibilities of adulthood. These children will enter society ill-equipped to function in structured environments, leading to widespread entitlement, decreased productivity, and a weakening of the social fabric.

RAISING THE NEXT DECLINE

The parallels between ineffective parenting today and historical societal declines are too stark to ignore. Sir John Glubb's analysis of societal collapse shows that when empires entered their final stages, family structures broke down, discipline was eroded, and comfort was prioritized over responsibility. Much like the latter days of Rome, where citizens became more focused on personal luxury than civic duty, today's permissive parenting reflects a broader cultural retreat from responsibility.

As Gen Z parents raise children without instilling a sense of duty, discipline, or resilience, they are contributing to the ongoing erosion of the societal foundations that once promoted growth and prosperity. This permissiveness not only damages individual families but also accelerates societal decline, as generations raised without a sense of responsibility or respect for authority are less able to contribute to the collective good.

THE SOCIETAL COST OF PERMISSIVE PARENTING

The consequences of permissive parenting are already being felt across various sectors of society. Employers are finding it increasingly difficult to manage young workers who expect rewards without merit, cannot handle constructive criticism, and lack the perseverance to overcome challenges. This entitlement is not only reducing workplace productivity but also creating a culture where standards of excellence and teamwork are eroded by individual fragility and self-interest.

Educational institutions, too, are struggling to manage students who are emotionally fragile and behaviorally problematic. Teachers report that students from permissive households often expect special treatment, react poorly to discipline, and resist the authority of educators. As these students move into adulthood, the larger societal institutions — businesses, government, and civic organizations — will face the challenge of integrating individuals who have never been held accountable.

A NEED FOR STRONGER PARENTING

Permissive parenting has become a widespread problem, exacerbated by the broader cultural emphasis on comfort, emotional validation, and avoiding conflict. Generation Z parents must recognize that by abdicating their responsibility to set boundaries and enforce discipline, they are raising children who are unprepared for adulthood. This failure is not just a family issue but a societal one, with far-reaching consequences that affect everything from education to the economy.

Parents must reclaim their role as authority figures, balancing love and support with the structure and discipline that children need to grow into responsible, resilient adults.

Setting clear boundaries, enforcing consequences, and allowing children to experience failure and adversity are essential steps toward breaking the cycle of entitlement and dependency. Only by doing so can we ensure that the next generation can face the challenges of adulthood and contributing meaningfully to society.

CHAPTER NINE

RISE OF THE KARENS

In the modern landscape of entitlement, the "Karen" and "Ken" phenomenon has emerged as a prominent cultural symbol of privilege, expectation, and societal breakdown. These characters—frequently depicted in viral videos demanding to "speak to the manager" over trivial issues—represent the epitome of inflated self-importance. Their behaviors are not entirely new but have been amplified by social media and consumer culture, where entitlement thrives. Though often associated with older generations, the rise of Karens and Kens reflects broader societal trends that link entitlement across generations, including the influence of Gen Z. This chapter explores how the entitlement mentality has infiltrated every age group, and how it reflects a deeper decline in societal values.

THE KAREN AND KEN PHENOMENON: ENTITLEMENT IN ACTION

The term "Karen" has become shorthand for individuals — predominantly middle-aged women — who feel entitled to special treatment and are quick to escalate minor issues into full-blown confrontations. Similarly, "Ken" refers to the male counterpart, though less frequently used. These viral caricatures are often shown berating customer service workers, calling the police over petty disputes, or asserting dominance in social situations. At their core, Karens and Kens embody a belief that their preferences and comfort are of paramount importance.

VIRAL VIDEOS OF KARENS

Social media platforms have become inundated with videos showcasing Karen and Ken behaviors in the wild. One prominent example is the 2020 "Central Park Karen" incident, where a woman falsely claimed that a Black man was threatening her after he politely asked her to leash her dog in accordance with park rules. This episode not only highlighted entitlement but also exposed the weaponization of victimhood, where Karens and Kens use their perceived authority or privilege to control or escalate otherwise mundane situations.

These viral moments often evoke a shared sense of frustration from viewers, yet they also reveal deeper societal issues. The behaviors of Karens and Kens are not just isolated incidents but are symptomatic of an entitlement culture that has permeated every aspect of public life. When minor inconveniences trigger explosive demands for preferential treatment, it underscores how fragile societal interactions have become in the face of personal entitlement.

THE PSYCHOLOGY OF ENTITLEMENT

Psychologically, the behavior of Karens and Kens stems from a sense of superiority and control. Social psychologists point to a strong link between entitlement and the need for dominance. These individuals often believe that their status—whether derived from race, socioeconomic standing, or sheer force of personality—grants them the right to demand exceptional treatment. They cannot tolerate being denied, and when confronted with minor discomforts, they lash out in an attempt to regain control.

This sense of entitlement is also deeply rooted in consumer culture. The mantra "the customer is always right" has long emboldened individuals to assert unreasonable demands. The rise of instant gratification, bolstered by the convenience of online shopping, has created a cultural expectation that every problem can and should be resolved to the individual's satisfaction—immediately and without inconvenience.

GEN Z'S INFLUENCE ON CONSUMER CULTURE AND ENTITLEMENT

While the Karen and Ken stereotype focuses on older individuals, there is an undeniable connection between Gen Z's consumer habits and the amplification of entitled behaviors. Gen Z, raised on digital platforms where instant feedback and rapid service are the norm, has inadvertently normalized a culture where every dissatisfaction—no matter how minor— must be addressed, and quickly.

ENTITLEMENT IN CONSUMER CULTURE

Gen Z's upbringing in a world where they can order food, buy products, or even cancel subscriptions with the click of a button has fostered expectations of immediacy and personal validation. Online platforms like Amazon or Uber Eats provide seamless, fast solutions to consumer needs, reinforcing the idea that delays or imperfections are unacceptable. While this convenience is a hallmark of modern technology, it also fuels a growing sense of entitlement, where patience and understanding take a backseat to immediate satisfaction.

This culture of entitlement has spread to older generations, influencing the behaviors of Boomers and Gen Xers. They too have come to expect swift resolutions in real-world interactions, expecting the same frictionless experience they encounter online. The Karen and Ken phenomenon is the result of this trickledown effect, where older generations adopt the instant gratification mindset of younger consumers and apply it to traditional service environments. The expectation that every demand should be met—whether reasonable or not—fuels public confrontations and exposes the depth of societal entitlement.

SOCIAL MEDIA AMPLIFICATION

Social media has exacerbated Karen and Ken behaviors by providing a platform for public grievances to go viral. Outrage culture, where individuals take to Twitter or TikTok to call out perceived wrongdoings, has encouraged confrontations that might have once remained private. As these incidents are shared and commented on, they gain traction, turning personal entitlement into public entertainment.

The accessibility of social media further entrenches this behavior by reinforcing the idea that complaining loudly enough will lead to a quick resolution. Karens and Kens, conscious of the power of public shaming, often escalate minor situations expecting companies or institutions will bow to the pressure of negative publicity. In this way, social media has become both a stage and an amplifier for entitled behavior.

THE KAREN/KEN CONNECTION TO GENERATIONAL DECLINE

While Karens and Kens are most often associated with older generations, their behaviors are emblematic of a larger societal issue that transcends age. The entitlement displayed by these individuals is a manifestation of a deeper cultural shift, where self-interest and personal comfort are prioritized over collective wellbeing. This widespread entitlement reflects the broader societal decline that has been observed throughout history.

ENTITLEMENT ACROSS GENERATIONS

Although Gen Z is frequently criticized for being entitled, the Karen and Ken phenomenon reveals that entitlement is not limited to younger people. Older generations, who once prided themselves on hard work and resilience, are now exhibiting the same self-centered behaviors. This generational convergence of entitlement illustrates how deeply ingrained this mindset has become. The constant demand for special treatment, regardless of age, signals a broader cultural shift away from values like humility, patience, and responsibility.

This societal entitlement mirrors the attitudes seen in the decline of previous civilizations. Historically, as societies became more prosperous, citizens grew more focused on personal comfort and luxury, leading to the erosion of discipline, resilience, and civic responsibility. The rise of Karens and Kens suggests that modern society is following a similar trajectory, where entitlement has become the norm, eroding social cohesion and weakening communal values.

RISK OF SOCIETAL STAGNATION

The proliferation of Karen and Ken behaviors signals a growing societal stagnation. When individuals are more focused on minor inconveniences and personal grievances than on contributing to the collective good, society risks falling into a state of complacency. This entitlement driven culture is reminiscent of the decline of empires such as Rome, where citizens prioritized personal luxury and comfort, contributing to the eventual collapse of the empire.

As entitlement spreads across generations, it threatens to weaken the social fabric, much like it did during the decline of historical empires. When self-interest and individual gratification overshadow communal responsibility, societies lose their ability to innovate, collaborate, and progress. The rise of Karens and Kens is not just a reflection of individual behaviors; it is a warning sign of a broader cultural and societal decay.

ENTITLEMENT RUN AMOK

The "Karen" and "Ken" phenomenon might be dismissed as a funny viral trend, but it's far from a joke. It's symptomatic of a far deeper rot—a culture of entitlement that stretches across generations and permeates every corner of society. What began as exaggerated portrayals of entitled, demanding individuals has become an all too real reflection of the society we live in, where personal demands and petty grievances are elevated above the common good.

If we don't put a stop to this growing entitlement, we'll see the same erosion of social stability that has brought down civilizations before us. History is full of examples where empires collapsed when personal comfort became more important than collective progress. We are on the same path, coddling self-centered complaints and individual privilege while ignoring the values that truly hold a society together—humility, resilience, and shared responsibility.

It's time to say enough. This culture of entitlement has gone unchecked for too long, and it's dragging us down. Society cannot function if every individual believes their personal whims trump the needs of the community. If we are to reverse this trend, we must abandon the obsession with individual privilege and refocus on the greater good. Only by fostering a culture that prioritizes community, responsibility, and grit can we halt this decline and ensure a stable, cohesive future. Entitlement is a luxury we can no longer afford.

A MESSAGE TO KARENS AND KENS: SOCIETY HAS HAD ENOUGH

Karens and Kens, it's time for a reality check. Your entitled, self-absorbed behavior has gone too far, and we're done bending to your will. Society has collectively decided that your tantrums, demands, and delusions of grandeur are no longer acceptable. You've strutted around, believing that your personal preferences and grievances should be catered to at every turn, but guess what? You're not special, and the world doesn't revolve around you.

Your days of throwing fits over trivial inconveniences and expecting everyone to jump when you snap your fingers are over. We've seen it all—the screaming at retail workers, the public meltdowns when you don't get your way, the relentless need to escalate every minor issue like you're royalty. Well, you're not. You're behaving like petulant children, and like children, it's time for you to be put in the corner.

Your entitled attitude isn't just embarrassing—it's destructive. It undermines the fabric of society, eroding decency, humility, and mutual respect. Your loud complaints, your threats to "call the manager," your belief that rules don't apply to you—it all stops now. Society isn't going to cater to your every whim anymore. You don't get special treatment, you don't make the rules, and no one is interested in your self-important demands.

We've had enough of your behavior, and it's time you faced the consequences. Like a spoiled child who's been indulged for far too long, you'll now find that no one is going to indulge you anymore. We'll tolerate your tantrums no more, and when you inevitably act out, we'll ignore you, sideline you, and leave you standing there alone, whining into the void. If you can't grow up, then you'll be left behind.

So, consider this your last warning: society has moved on, and your entitled ways are no longer welcome. Adapt, grow up, or fade into irrelevance. The choice is yours, but the world won't wait for you to catch up.

CHAPTER TEN

BREAKING THE CYCLE OF ENTITLEMENT

The entitlement epidemic, which has taken root across multiple generations, has profoundly disrupted family dynamics, educational institutions, workplaces, and society at large. It fosters a culture where personal desires and grievances are prioritized over responsibility and communal wellbeing. To counter these destructive trends, we must implement bold and practical solutions that emphasize discipline, personal accountability, and societal reform. By shifting focus toward resilience, respect for authority, and the common good, we can restore balance and build a society that values growth over comfort, responsibility over-indulgence, and collective strength over individual entitlement.

REINFORCING DISCIPLINE IN THE FAMILY

Family is the first place where entitlement takes hold, and it's also where it must be dismantled. Parents need to reclaim their role as authority figures rather than enablers of their children's whims. This means establishing clear boundaries and teaching children from a young age that actions have consequences. Parents must stop bending to every demand, instead enforcing rules, expectations, and responsibilities that foster independence. Children need to contribute to the household, learn the value of hard work, and understand that privileges are earned, not given.

The trend of allowing adult children to linger in dependency must end. Parents should push their grown children toward financial and personal independence by setting firm expectations for rent, bills, and responsibilities. The goal is to prepare them for the realities of life, not shelter them from it. A return to disciplined parenting will go a long way in curbing entitlement at its roots.

RESHAPING EDUCATIONAL SYSTEMS FOR ACCOUNTABILITY

Educational institutions, which have increasingly become breeding grounds for entitlement, need a cultural overhaul. The focus must shift away from creating comfortable, stress-free environments toward fostering intellectual rigor, personal accountability, and resilience. Safe spaces and trigger warnings, while rooted in good intentions, too often reinforce fragility. Instead, schools should challenge students to engage with difficult ideas, learn how to handle discomfort, and develop the critical thinking skills necessary for real-world success.

Discipline should be reintroduced into the educational framework. Students must be held accountable for their actions and performance, learning that failure and hardship are part of the growth process. By emphasizing accountability and resilience over emotional accommodation, schools can help reverse the entitlement trend and prepare students for the demands of adulthood.

PROMOTING RESPONSIBILITY IN THE WORKPLACE

In the workplace, entitlement has manifested in unrealistic expectations, a lack of work ethic, and a resistance to authority. Employers must push back against this by reinforcing a culture of meritocracy, where rewards and advancements are earned through hard work and results, not handed out based on demands or perceived entitlements.

Workplaces should prioritize performance-based evaluations and encourage employees to take ownership of their roles. Clear consequences for poor performance or unprofessional behavior should be implemented, and respect for authority and organizational rules should be nonnegotiable. Additionally, employers should foster an environment where resilience and adaptability are valued, reminding employees that work is not about personal comfort, but about contributing to a collective goal.

SOCIETAL REFORM: PRIORITIZING COMMUNITY OVER INDIVIDUALISM

The entitlement epidemic has flourished in a culture that prioritizes individual comfort and personal expression over community wellbeing. To counter this, society must shift back toward valuing collective responsibility and civic duty. This means rejecting the notion that every personal grievance deserves attention and reminding individuals that they are part of a larger society with shared responsibilities.

Public policies should reflect this change in values, promoting personal accountability and discouraging dependency. Welfare systems, while necessary for those truly in need, should be structured to encourage self-sufficiency and responsibility, not foster long-term reliance. Community service and civic engagement should be encouraged at all levels, reminding individuals that their actions affect others, and that societal progress depends on shared effort, not individual entitlement.

BREAKING THE CYCLE OF ENTITLEMENT

The culture of entitlement we see today is not a sudden phenomenon—it has evolved over decades, with influences stretching from parenting styles to social programs that inadvertently reward dependency. Reversing these trends requires a comprehensive approach, tackling both cultural and systemic factors. The following solutions are designed to address entitlement at its core, by restoring values like resilience, accountability, and respect for authority. These are the foundations necessary to build a stronger, more cohesive society.

1. Mandatory national service to instill resilience

One of the most effective ways to address the erosion of resilience is through a program of mandatory national service. This would require young adults to engage in meaningful service to the country, helping them build character and contribute to the greater good. National service programs could range from military service to civil initiatives like healthcare assistance, infrastructure development, and education.

Mandatory national service would force young adults to step out of their comfort zones, confront challenges head-on, and develop a strong work ethic. By working alongside peers from diverse backgrounds, participants would gain valuable lessons in teamwork, perseverance, and adaptability — qualities that are sorely lacking in a generation that has been raised in a culture of instant gratification. The mental toughness and resilience cultivated in these programs would not only prepare individuals for their personal futures but also contribute to societal strength.

Resilience is cultivated not in ease, but in adversity. In a world where convenience has become the norm, there is limited exposure to real challenges that test the spirit and build perseverance. National service programs would provide young people with structured challenges—ranging from the physical demands of military training to the emotional demands of working in underserved communities. These experiences foster both grit and empathy, preparing them for life's inevitable setbacks.

National service brings people together in a way few other experiences can. Whether serving in the military, teaching in underserved communities, or working on conservation projects, young adults would develop a shared sense of purpose and responsibility. This could help bridge the widening divides in society by fostering a stronger sense of national identity and solidarity.

In a time when polarization has reached unprecedented levels, shared experiences have the power to heal. National service offers the opportunity to break out of echo chambers, exposing individuals to people with different backgrounds, cultures, and perspectives. By working toward common goals, they not only learn to respect differences but also realize the strength of unity—something our society desperately needs.

For too long, individual achievement and personal comfort have been prioritized over collective responsibility. Mandatory national service would emphasize that individuals are part of something larger than themselves, countering the excessive individualism that has fueled the entitlement mentality. It would remind young people that personal sacrifices are sometimes necessary for the greater good.

The "me-first" mentality has led to a decline in social cohesion. National service programs would act as a corrective measure, shifting the emphasis back to community. Participants would be confronted with the idea that their actions—or inactions—impact others. The experience would cultivate humility and an understanding of the importance of contributing to something beyond one's self-interest.

All young adults, upon completing high school or reaching the age of 18, would be required to commit to two years of national service. This could include military service, environmental conservation, healthcare assistance, or social services like mentoring or education programs. A two-year program ensures that participants have enough time to gain a meaningful experience that leaves a lasting impact on their character.

To accommodate individual skills and interests, the program would offer various service tracks. This ensures that each participant finds a meaningful role while contributing to the nation. For example, someone interested in education might teach in underfunded schools, while another might contribute to building infrastructure in rural areas. By providing options, we ensure that participants are engaged and motivated, making their service not just an obligation but an opportunity for personal growth.

2. Parental education programs to rebuild traditional family values

A critical component of reversing the entitlement trend lies in reforming parenting practices. The way children are raised directly impacts the kind of adults they become. Permissive parenting styles, where boundaries are often weak or nonexistent, contribute to the "I'm special" syndrome that fuels entitlement. Parental education programs can address this issue by helping parents establish clear boundaries, enforce discipline, and promote resilience in their children.

Parents need to understand that effective parenting involves both love and firm boundaries. Children thrive when they know what is expected of them and when consequences for poor behavior are consistent. Parental education programs emphasize the importance of structure and discipline, teaching parents how to set rules that guide their children toward maturity and responsibility.

Boundaries create a sense of security. Children need to know where the lines are drawn—it helps them understand expectations and consequences. Without these boundaries, children grow up with a skewed sense of freedom, believing they can act without accountability. Parental education programs would focus on the concept of "tough love"—being nurturing while setting and maintaining consistent rules that teach respect and responsibility.

Parents should be educated on how to balance nurturing with holding their children to high standards. Having high expectations does not mean being harsh or unkind; rather, it means teaching children to strive for excellence and accountability while knowing they have their parents' unwavering support. This approach encourages a growth mindset, where children learn to see challenges as opportunities for growth rather than as obstacles to avoid.

The key is to cultivate resilience and ambition. Children who are encouraged to aim high, while being supported emotionally, are more likely to develop confidence and perseverance. Parental education would help caregivers strike the right balance, making sure their children know they are loved, but also that they have a responsibility to push themselves and contribute meaningfully to the world.

These parental education programs could be offered through schools, community centers, and online platforms.

Workshops, led by experienced educators, psychologists, and community leaders, would provide parents with practical strategies for raising disciplined, resilient children. By equipping parents with these tools, we can break the cycle of permissiveness and foster a generation that understands the importance of effort, responsibility, and respect for others.

These workshops would be tailored to the challenges parents face today—addressing issues like screen time, effective discipline, and fostering independence. By creating community support structures, we empower parents to share experiences and learn from each other, building a network that helps families thrive.

3. **Shifting away from entitlement programs that reward dependency**

Entitlement programs, while originally designed to support those in need, have in many cases contributed to long-term dependency and a culture of complacency. Reforming these programs to focus on independence and self-sufficiency is critical in combating entitlement.

Entitlement programs should include work or community service requirements for able-bodied recipients. By linking benefits to participation in society, individuals are encouraged to contribute to their communities while receiving temporary support. This approach fosters a sense of responsibility and dignity.

By requiring active participation, entitlement programs would shift from being a "handout" to a "hand up." Work requirements could be tailored to an individual's capabilities, ensuring that those who are genuinely in need receive help while also contributing in some capacity. This fosters personal accountability and reduces the stigma often associated with receiving public support.

Entitlement programs should focus on empowering individuals to develop skills that enable them to become self-reliant. This could involve offering job training, education programs, and career development resources as part of the benefits. The goal should always be to help individuals transition from dependency to independence, giving them the tools to thrive on their own.

Incentives for education and job training would help recipients break free from the cycle of poverty and dependency. These programs would focus on upskilling—equipping individuals with modern skills that align with workforce demands. By investing in human potential, we create a more self-sufficient and productive society.

To prevent long-term dependency, entitlement benefits should be time limited. While temporary assistance is essential for those facing hardships, prolonged reliance on government support erodes personal responsibility and ambition. Time limits, paired with robust job placement services, will encourage individuals to take active steps toward independence.

Time limited benefits create urgency, prompting individuals to take advantage of support services, including job placement and training programs. This approach motivates recipients to engage in their personal development actively and reduces the risk of becoming complacent.

4. Reforming education to foster discipline and accountability

The education system plays a pivotal role in shaping societal values. Schools must become places that emphasize discipline, hard work, and accountability — countering the culture of entitlement and the overinflated sense of individual specialness.

Schools should reintroduce character education programs that focus on responsibility, respect, and empathy. Civics education should also be expanded to teach students about their roles as citizens and the importance of respecting laws and authority. Such programs would instill values of cooperation, service, and accountability.

Character education is essential to fostering well-rounded individuals. By teaching values like empathy and respect, schools can help counteract the self-centeredness that entitlement breeds. Civics education would help students understand their role within a larger community, emphasizing their responsibilities as citizens and community members.

The practice of giving participation trophies has created a generation of individuals who expect rewards without genuine achievement. Schools should return to rewarding actual effort and excellence, reinforcing the idea that success is earned, not given.

Recognizing true effort helps cultivate ambition and resilience. It encourages students to strive for success rather than expect recognition simply for showing up. By rewarding hard work, schools reinforce the importance of perseverance and dedication, laying the groundwork for future success.

Students should learn to engage in respectful debate and constructive disagreement. Schools can help counter the rise of cancel culture by teaching students how to listen to and respect differing opinions. This fosters intellectual resilience and a more mature approach to conflict resolution.

The ability to engage in civil discourse is a crucial life skill. Schools must create environments where differing opinions are discussed openly, teaching students to disagree without disrespect. This not only prepares students for the complexities of adult life but also helps foster a culture of mutual respect and understanding.

Schools must set clear rules for behavior and enforce them consistently. Respect for teachers and authority figures should be a nonnegotiable aspect of school culture, reinforcing the idea that actions have consequences.

Clear, consistent rules help establish a sense of order and safety within schools. When students understand the expectations and the consequences for misbehavior, they are more likely to behave responsibly. Schools must make it clear that respect for authority is fundamental to a productive learning environment.

Teachers need the backing of parents and school administrators to maintain discipline in the classroom. Effective disciplinary policies that involve both school and home can create a consistent environment of accountability, helping students learn the importance of self-control and respect for authority.

Teachers often struggle with enforcing discipline when they lack support from parents or administrators. By ensuring that teachers have the backing they need, schools create a unified front that reinforces the values of respect and accountability.

Discipline should be seen not as punitive, but as a tool for growth and character development.

5. Reinstating respect for authority

Restoring respect for authority is essential for maintaining social order. Whether in the form of law enforcement, educators, or public servants, authority figures play a crucial role in ensuring the safety and stability of society.

Law enforcement agencies should expand community policing efforts, working closely with residents to solve problems and build relationships. By humanizing police officers and integrating them into the community, trust can be restored, and respect for law enforcement can be rebuilt.

Community policing brings law enforcement and citizens together as partners. By being visible and approachable, officers can break down barriers, reduce misunderstandings, and build positive relationships. This approach emphasizes that law enforcement is a part of the community, not apart from it.

Public education campaigns focused on the vital role law enforcement plays in maintaining order can help reshape perceptions. These campaigns should emphasize the challenges officers face and the importance of their work in keeping communities safe.

By educating the public on the complexities and challenges of policing, we can foster greater empathy and respect. Understanding the sacrifices that law enforcement officers make can shift public perceptions and rebuild the trust that has been eroded in recent years.

By requiring young people to participate in community service, we can foster a sense of responsibility and respect for public servants. These programs allow individuals to see firsthand the work that goes into maintaining a functioning society, promoting a greater appreciation for authority figures.

Community service exposes individuals to the realities of the work done by authority figures and public servants. By engaging in community improvement projects, young people learn to appreciate the value of service and the importance of maintaining social structures.

Highlighting positive role models within law enforcement, education, and public service can shift the narrative around authority figures. Public campaigns that feature these role models can help inspire younger generations to respect those who serve the community and enforce the rules.

Role models provide tangible examples of what it means to serve with integrity and dedication. By showcasing the best of law enforcement, education, and public service, we inspire future generations to view authority as a positive force and something worthy of respect.

A PATH FORWARD TO STABILITY AND STRENGTH

The entitlement crisis that has weakened modern society can be addressed with the right combination of personal responsibility, discipline, and respect for authority. The solutions presented—mandatory national service, parental education, entitlement reform, educational reform, and restoring respect for authority—provide a roadmap for reversing these damaging trends.

Breaking the cycle of entitlement will require bold action and a commitment to reshaping societal values. By focusing on resilience, discipline, and accountability, we can create a society that values hard work, respect, and community, ensuring a stronger future for all.

CHAPTER ELEVEN

The Great Reset

The entitlement and fragility that have become pervasive in modern society have deep, generational roots, rooted in years of misguided policies, cultural shifts, and a celebration of the self that has stripped us of our collective strength. To correct these destructive tendencies, we must fundamentally rethink the societal pillars that have shaped this environment. This chapter presents actionable solutions aimed at restoring accountability, promoting resilience, and rebuilding societal values that prioritize collective wellbeing over individual comfort. It is time to replace the destructive hyper individualism that dominates our culture with a framework that values community, shared goals, and a willingness to overcome discomfort for the greater good.

1. **Implement Societal Policies That Emphasize Personal Accountability and Resilience**

One of the most effective ways to combat entitlement is through policy reforms that shift the focus from dependency to self-reliance and personal responsibility.

Welfare Reform: The current welfare systems, while providing critical support for those in immediate need, are failing at long-term upliftment. Too often, these programs foster a cycle of dependency that drains societal resources while trapping individuals in situations that limit their growth. Reform is necessary to create a system where assistance is temporary, and self-improvement is central. By incorporating work requirements, educational programs, and skill development into welfare, we can help recipients reclaim their independence. Wisconsin's model of welfare-to-work, with its combination of training and incentives, should serve as an example nationwide, proving that empowerment through opportunity is far superior to indefinite assistance.

Shift from Assistance to Empowerment: Welfare must focus on equipping individuals to succeed independently. Rather than simply offering financial aid, programs should emphasize training in critical life skills, financial literacy, and job preparedness. Individuals who receive support must be challenged to better themselves and ultimately contribute meaningfully to society. The system should encourage short-term support to enable people to transition to a life where they are providers, not merely recipients.

Mandatory National Service: As previously discussed, one of the most impactful reforms would be the introduction of a mandatory national service program for all young adults. Nations like Israel and Switzerland have reaped immense benefits from such programs — developing a culture of resilience, discipline, and civic responsibility. A mandatory two-year period of national service, whether military, civil, or community focused, would expose young adults to real-world challenges and create an understanding of the value of service. The experiences gained during this time would teach discipline, resourcefulness, and the importance of community — traits currently eroded by a society that places far too much emphasis on personal comfort.

Building Civic Unity: National service does more than prepare individuals; it builds bridges. Young people from different backgrounds working side-by-side fosters unity and reduces social division. It becomes a shared experience that binds citizens together, building a society where the needs of the many are recognized as being more important than the whims of the few.

2. Legislation to Curb Social Media's Influence

Social media has acted as an accelerant for entitlement and emotional fragility. It has distorted our culture, transforming our perceptions of success, beauty, and what it means to lead a meaningful life. The unchecked influence of these platforms must be addressed to preserve mental wellbeing and societal harmony.

Mental Health Responsibility: Social media companies have allowed their platforms to devolve into toxic environments that breed anxiety, depression, and dissatisfaction. They must be held accountable for the mental health impact of their platforms. Legislation, like Denmark's, that requires influencers to disclose image editing is a step forward, but more must be done. Enforcing global standards for realistic representation would mitigate the damaging effects of idealized and manipulated content.

Realistic Content Requirements: Platforms must be mandated to promote transparency. By holding content creators responsible for perpetuating unrealistic expectations, we can reduce the pressure to conform to distorted ideals of success, beauty, and worth. The focus must shift from superficial validation to deeper, more meaningful growth.

Promote Digital Detox Days: Governments should take the lead in promoting national digital detox initiatives. These detoxes could take place quarterly, where schools, businesses, and other institutions actively encourage disconnection from social media. Research suggests that unplugging even for a single day leads to improved mental health and productivity. These initiatives are vital to countering the addiction to validation and instant gratification, fostering a healthier relationship with technology.

3. Introduce Resilience-Building Programs in Schools and Workplaces

Education has shifted away from preparing students for adversity, instead prioritizing shielding them from discomfort. This is an unsustainable approach that leaves young people ill-equipped to handle life's inevitable challenges.

Mandatory Resilience Education: Schools must introduce resilience focused courses that teach problem-solving, emotional intelligence, and adaptability. The Finnish education system — one of the best globally — has consistently shown that students who learn to manage failure and overcome obstacles achieve far better outcomes in both academics and life. Resilience is not innate; it must be taught, nurtured, and reinforced. By confronting students with challenges, we prepare them to navigate a world that does not cater to their every need.

Developing Problem-Solvers, Not Avoiders: Emphasizing resilience is about shifting mindsets. Schools should teach students to approach adversity as an opportunity to grow, not as something to be feared or avoided. This is a foundational shift that will prepare students to confront real-world problems with confidence and ingenuity, creating generations that see obstacles as steppingstones rather than barriers.

Shift the Workplace Mindset: The modern workplace often prioritizes comfort at the expense of growth. Safe spaces and excessive mental health days may provide temporary relief, but they also risk creating environments that foster avoidance. Instead, workplaces should implement resilience and stress management workshops to provide tools that help employees manage adversity. Studies have shown that resilience training can significantly reduce burnout and improve productivity, ensuring that employees are prepared to face challenges head-on, rather than shy away from them.

4. Overhaul Social Media and Content Creation Models

The very algorithms that drive social media engagement are often responsible for promoting divisive, entitlement focused content. To correct this, platforms must be restructured to prioritize positive, educational, and community building interactions.

Prioritize Constructive Content: Social media companies must reform their algorithms to promote constructive, community-oriented content. The current model, which rewards outrage and division, has bred a culture of hostility and hyper individualism. Governments must work with technology companies to overhaul these algorithms, prioritizing content that brings people together and fosters intellectual growth.

Learning from Success: Platforms like YouTube have taken initial steps to reduce sensationalist content in favor of longform educational material. Expanding this approach is critical across all major platforms, encouraging healthier, more enriching interactions that contribute to personal and societal wellbeing.

Encouraging Shared Values: One of the most damaging byproducts of social media has been the amplification of identity politics. Encouraging people to identify primarily through victimhood or perceived oppression divides rather than unites. Social media and content models must be transformed to emphasize shared human experiences, values, and collective goals. Highlighting commonality fosters social cohesion and reduces the conflict bred by divisiveness.

The entitlement and dependency trends we have explored are unsustainable. They mirror the patterns of decline seen in past civilizations—such as Rome and the British Empire. A society that overvalues comfort, gratification, and individual entitlement at the expense of collective wellbeing is doomed to stagnate and collapse. The Great Reset is not a suggestion; it is a necessity.

We are at a pivotal moment. Each year that passes without decisive action deepens these destructive tendencies. Radical reforms are needed to create a culture that values resilience, accountability, and community. This requires not just government intervention, but an overhaul of our societal expectations—from how we raise our children to how we consume information and perceive success.

A CALL TO REBUILD

The solutions presented throughout this book culminate in a call for collective action. The Great Reset is not the responsibility of governments or institutions alone; it requires every individual, family, and community to play an active role. Parents must instill discipline, educators must teach resilience, and governments must regulate industries that contribute to societal decline.

This is not a call to return to an idealized past, but a blueprint for a future that learns from history's mistakes. A future that embraces strength, accountability, and community as core values. We stand at a crossroads: either continue down the path of entitlement and fragility or choose to build a culture that is grounded in resilience and shared responsibility. The choice is ours, and the time to act is now.

CHAPTER TWELVE

DEALING WITH SNOWFLAKES, KENS, AND KARENS

The rise of the "snowflake" mentality—characterized by fragility, entitlement, and an aversion to accountability—has become a visible and frustrating phenomenon in everyday life. Whether it manifests in the workplace, public spaces, or social interactions, individuals often encounter people who display an inflated sense of self-importance, easily take offense, and make demands that undermine mutual respect and social cohesion. These behaviors, while commonly associated with younger generations, have also infiltrated older groups, giving rise to what has been popularly termed "Karen" or "Ken" behavior— a sense of entitlement expressed through demands for special treatment or exaggerated grievances.

This chapter explores how we can effectively respond when faced with such behaviors. It goes beyond merely confronting these individuals and focuses on practical strategies for fostering a culture that rejects complacency, encourages personal responsibility, and reclaims mutual respect in social interactions.

RECOGNIZING THE BEHAVIOR: WHAT ARE WE DEALING WITH?

Before considering how to respond, it is crucial to recognize the behavior at hand. A "snowflake" moment often involves disproportionate emotional responses to minor inconveniences, an insistence on being treated as exceptional, or outrage over perceived slights that conflict with personal sensitivities. In public, this behavior might involve overreacting to perceived inefficiencies, demanding special treatment, or attempting to silence opposing viewpoints.

"Ken" or "Karen" behavior often mirrors this but with a more confrontational, entitlement fueled edge—public outbursts, complaints over trivial matters, or demands to speak to management for the slightest perceived offense. These individuals feel wronged, not because of any genuine injustice, but because their personal comfort or convenience has been compromised. Recognizing these behaviors as symptomatic of a broader cultural problem is the first step in determining an appropriate response.

RESPONDING WITH FIRMNESS AND CIVILITY

When encountering "snowflake" behavior, the impulse to respond with equal frustration or passive avoidance may feel natural, but it is rarely effective. Instead, the most constructive response balances firmness with civility. Rather than indulging the behavior or caving to unreasonable demands, one should respond by setting clear boundaries while maintaining composure. This approach communicates that, while their feelings or concerns may be acknowledged, entitlement and overreaction will not dictate the situation.

For instance, in a workplace setting where an individual demands special treatment, calmly but firmly reinforcing company policy or shared team values can effectively reset expectations. A response might be something like: "I understand that this situation may feel frustrating, but we all need to follow the same procedures to keep things fair and efficient." The key is to maintain authority without engaging in the same emotional intensity that characterizes their behavior.

In public spaces or service environments, responding to "Karen" or "Ken" behavior requires similar restraint. A calm refusal to acquiesce to excessive demands, combined with a restatement of policies or norms, communicates that their behavior is neither justified nor rewarded. Politeness, coupled with an unyielding commitment to fairness, diffuses the situation and discourages future entitlement driven outbursts.

THE ROLE OF ACCOUNTABILITY: LETTING CONSEQUENCES SPEAK

An essential response to this behavior lies in reestablishing the value of accountability. When "snowflakes" or "Karens" act out without facing meaningful consequences, the behavior is likely to be repeated. Instituting clear, fair consequences for actions—whether through workplace discipline, public rebuke, or legal channels in extreme cases—reinforces the idea that actions have repercussions.

For example, companies can foster a culture that discourages entitlement by promoting personal responsibility and setting transparent consequences for inappropriate behavior. This could mean implementing policies that ensure customer complaints are addressed without rewarding entitled or abusive behavior. Similarly, in personal interactions, making it clear that certain behaviors are unacceptable—by calmly disengaging or refusing to validate exaggerated grievances—helps assert boundaries.

In cases where legal intervention may be necessary, such as public disturbances or harassment, involving authorities when appropriate can act as a deterrent. However, accountability can also take simpler forms: social disapproval or being politely but firmly corrected in the moment can be enough to check entitled behavior.

CHALLENGING THE CULTURE OF VICTIMHOOD

A significant driver behind the "snowflake" phenomenon is the broader culture of victimhood that often elevates personal grievances into matters of injustice. When individuals prioritize their own feelings over shared responsibilities or claim oppression in situations that merely reflect the challenges of everyday life, society suffers a breakdown in its capacity for mutual respect and cooperation.

The antidote to this culture is fostering resilience and a mindset of personal responsibility. Encouraging individuals, especially in younger generations, to adopt a mindset that prizes grit over grievance, and perseverance over protest, is key. In responding to individuals caught in a "snowflake" mentality, we can promote these values by challenging their narratives of victimhood with questions that encourage reflection: "Is this issue really as big as you're making it out to be?" or "How might you handle this differently next time to avoid such frustration?" Engaging people to think critically about their reactions, rather than simply indulging or dismissing them, can lead to more productive outcomes.

BUILDING A CULTURE OF MUTUAL RESPECT

Perhaps the most effective long-term response to the snowflake and entitlement mentality is to actively build a culture of mutual respect. While we cannot singlehandedly change an entire generation's mindset, we can influence the spaces we inhabit—whether those are professional, social, or familial—by modeling behavior that values personal responsibility, civility, and shared accountability.

Encouraging open dialogue, promoting balanced leadership, and rewarding behaviors that contribute to the common good are all practical steps toward this goal. For example, in the workplace, cultivating an environment where team members are expected to carry their weight, recognize their limitations, and contribute to collective goals can reduce the incidence of entitled behavior. Socially fostering respectful discussions where differing viewpoints are acknowledged but not validated helps to establish an expectation of civil discourse.

When encountering entitled or "snowflake" behavior in personal or public settings, demonstrating respect and composure—while firmly refusing to indulge unreasonable demands—sets a standard for how others should interact. Respect for others does not mean capitulating to entitlement; rather, it involves holding people accountable to the same standards expected of everyone.

REJECTING THE "KAREN" MENTALITY: THE POWER OF SOCIAL RECALIBRATION

Finally, rejecting the "Karen" and "Ken" mentality requires a collective recalibration of social norms. This recalibration will only happen when enough people reject entitlement driven behavior and demand a higher standard of conduct. We can contribute to this recalibration through everyday actions: refusing to normalize temper tantrums in public, challenging coworkers or family members who act entitled, and supporting businesses or institutions that uphold fairness and responsibility.

The road ahead requires effort on both individual and collective levels. By consistently demanding better—from ourselves and from others—we can slowly begin to reverse the trend of entitlement, victimhood, and societal fragility. The goal is not just to curtail these behaviors but to foster a culture where resilience, accountability, and respect are valued and practiced across all generations.

TOWARD A BETTER FUTURE

The response to snowflakes, Kens, and Karens must be grounded in firm boundaries, a refusal to indulge entitlement, and a commitment to rebuilding a culture of mutual respect. While encountering these behaviors may frustrate, the most powerful response is one that elevates societal expectations and holds individuals accountable for their actions. By demanding better, we can rebuild the values that foster resilience and cohesion, helping to restore a sense of purpose, responsibility, and dignity in our everyday interactions.

CHAPTER THIRTEEN

THE RISE OF DEI BUREAUCRACIES

In the past decade, Diversity, Equity, and Inclusion (DEI) initiatives have transformed from small-scale programs aimed at promoting fair treatment into expansive bureaucratic structures with significant influence over hiring, promotion, and organizational culture. Originally conceived to address issues of discrimination and foster fairness, these initiatives have gradually shifted under the influence of political pressure, legal mandates, and corporate self-interest. DEI departments have flourished to the point where they now act as gatekeepers of what is considered acceptable thought and behavior within institutions.

This transformation has led to the emergence of an ideological orthodoxy. Within this framework, dissent is often swiftly labeled as intolerance or bigotry, even when objections are rooted in reasoned critiques or alternative perspectives. This new dynamic has resulted in environments where merit and competence are sometimes subordinated to identity categories, and those who question the efficacy or fairness of DEI policies may risk professional ostracism or worse.

THE UNINTENDED CONSEQUENCES OF DEI POLICIES

While DEI initiatives aim to address important issues like discrimination and inequality, their widespread application has produced several unintended consequences that often undermine their original goals.

1. **Erosion of Meritocracy:** One of the most prominent criticisms of DEI initiatives is the erosion of meritocratic principles. By placing identity factors—such as race, gender, or sexual orientation—above qualifications and competence, these programs risk rewarding mediocrity or inefficiency while sidelining the most capable individuals. This erosion of merit is particularly damaging in sectors where high performance and specialized skills are critical, such as healthcare, education, and business.

For example, in healthcare, prioritizing identity characteristics over qualifications could mean that a more competent doctor or nurse is overlooked in favor of a less qualified candidate who fulfills a diversity quota. In educational settings, the appointment of teachers or administrators based primarily on identity, rather than competence or experience, can lead to a decline in educational quality, impacting students who rely on skilled educators to shape their futures.

2. **Stifling of Open Dialogue:** DEI bureaucracies often promote a rigid ideological framework that discourages open discussion. In many organizations, questioning DEI principles or critiquing their implementation is tantamount to career suicide. Any pushback can lead to accusations of insensitivity, racism, or a lack of commitment to the organizational culture.

Consider a workplace scenario where an employee raises concerns about the implementation of mandatory unconscious bias training. This individual may be viewed not as someone contributing valuable feedback, but rather as a dissenter challenging the core values of the organization. Such a culture of fear silences productive conversations and prevents nuanced discussions about the tradeoffs and unintended consequences of these policies, ultimately leading to a lack of progress or improvement.

3. **Fostering Division:** Although DEI programs ostensibly seek to promote inclusivity, they often inadvertently foster division by emphasizing group identity over individual merit. When individuals are continuously categorized based on immutable characteristics such as race or gender, it can lead to feelings of tokenism, alienation, and even resentment.

For instance, some employees may feel that their achievements are overshadowed by assumptions that they were hired to fulfill a diversity quota. This diminishes their sense of accomplishment and can create friction between colleagues, undermining the goal of fostering an inclusive and cooperative workplace. Moreover, emphasizing group identities can reinforce stereotypes and deepen group-based resentment, perpetuating the very divisions that DEI programs were intended to eliminate.

4. **Bureaucratic Bloat and Inefficiency:** The rapid expansion of DEI offices has led to significant bureaucratic bloat in many institutions. DEI departments, tasked with monitoring, regulating, and enforcing standards, often drain resources without delivering meaningful results.

For example, large corporations and universities have increasingly employed numerous DEI officers and consultants. These positions often come with considerable salaries but may not necessarily add value to the institution's core mission. This allocation of resources—time, money, and personnel—can detract from more productive endeavors, such as enhancing services, improving operational efficiency, or investing in the professional development of employees.

SURVIVING DEI BUREAUCRACIES: STRATEGIES FOR INDIVIDUALS

For individuals working within organizations that have fully embraced DEI agendas, navigating the landscape can be challenging. It is essential to develop strategies for maintaining professional integrity while avoiding unnecessary conflicts that could jeopardize career progression or social standing. Below are some practical approaches:

1. **Focus on Excellence and Results:** The most effective counter to ideological rigidity is consistently delivering high quality work. By focusing on results and demonstrating competence, individuals can insulate themselves from accusations of noncompliance or disloyalty to DEI objectives. When your performance is irrefutable, it becomes more difficult for organizations to penalize you for not fully aligning with DEI orthodoxy.

For example, if you're in a sales role, let your numbers speak for themselves. Exceptional performance metrics and client satisfaction can act as a buffer against political pressures. Similarly, in academia, publishing high quality research and demonstrating excellence in teaching can help protect against ideological conformity pressures.

2. **Learn the Language but Don't Internalize It:** It is important to understand the vocabulary and frameworks promoted by DEI agendas to navigate bureaucratic environments without drawing undue attention. Familiarize yourself with terms like "microaggressions," "intersectionality," and "privilege," but resist internalizing them if they conflict with your beliefs.

Adopting a pragmatic approach—acknowledging these concepts without becoming beholden to them—can help you maintain your values while avoiding unnecessary confrontations. For example, during meetings or workshops, use the language as a tool to signal understanding, but don't let it compromise your fundamental principles or decision-making processes.

3. **Pick Your Battles:** In highly charged environments, picking your battles is crucial. Not every disagreement with DEI policies warrants vocal opposition. Reserve your objections for situations where the policies directly impact performance, fairness, or institutional integrity.

For example, you might choose to remain silent during a general DEI workshop but speak out if a policy is implemented that directly affects your ability to complete your job effectively. Knowing when to speak out and when to stay silent can preserve your credibility, minimize conflict, and help you avoid burnout.

4. **Build Alliances with Like Minded Individuals:** You are not alone in navigating DEI driven bureaucracies. Building alliances with likeminded colleagues can provide support and foster environments where open dialogue and alternative perspectives are valued.

For instance, informal networks or "affinity groups" of employees who share concerns about the impact of DEI policies can help create a support system. These groups may allow for discreet discussions and shared strategies for managing the pressures of conforming to DEI mandates, providing emotional and professional solidarity.

5. **Document Everything:** In environments where accusations of bias or noncompliance can be weaponized, it's crucial to document interactions and decisions meticulously. Keeping detailed records can protect against false claims and provide evidence in cases where DEI policies lead to unfair treatment.

For example, after meetings, consider writing a summary of what was discussed, decisions made, and any actions you were directed to take. If disagreements arise, this documentation serves as a factual basis to support your position.

CHALLENGING DEI BUREAUCRACIES: INSTITUTIONAL SOLUTIONS

While individuals can develop personal strategies for surviving DEI driven environments, broader institutional reforms are necessary to challenge the worst excesses of DEI bureaucracies and restore balance. Below are some strategies for organizations to consider:

1. **Reasserting the Primacy of Merit:** Institutions must reassert the importance of meritocracy in decision-making processes, particularly in hiring, promotions, and rewards. While diversity is a valuable goal, it should not come at the expense of excellence.

For example, an organization might revise its hiring practices to ensure that while a diverse pool of candidates is encouraged, the final decision is based solely on qualifications and the ability to contribute effectively to the organization. By ensuring that merit remains the primary criterion for advancement, institutions can maintain their competitive edge and ensure fairness.

2. **Encouraging Open Dialogue:** Organizations should foster environments where diverse viewpoints can be discussed openly without fear of retribution. Creating spaces for healthy debate and alternative perspectives ensures that DEI initiatives are scrutinized and refined

over time, making them more effective and less dogmatic.

For instance, leadership could hold regular town hall meetings where employees are invited to voice both support for and concerns about DEI policies. A culture that encourages questions and values all perspectives will yield more robust and inclusive outcomes.

3. **Regularly Evaluating DEI Outcomes:** Rather than assuming DEI policies are beneficial simply because they exist, organizations should regularly evaluate their impact on productivity, workplace culture, and fairness. Transparent reporting on DEI outcomes — including both successes and failures — will allow for necessary course corrections and reduce the risk of creating a stagnant, unaccountable bureaucracy.

Organizations could implement regular surveys to gauge employee sentiment regarding DEI initiatives and measure specific metrics, such as employee retention, performance outcomes, and job satisfaction across different identity groups. By assessing these outcomes, institutions can adapt their DEI programs to ensure they are genuinely contributing to the wellbeing and efficiency of the workplace.

4. **Avoiding Tokenism:** One of the key dangers of DEI agendas is the temptation to engage in tokenism —

making superficial or symbolic gestures toward diversity without addressing deeper institutional issues. Organizations must resist the urge to use DEI as a form of public relations or virtue signaling and instead focus on substantive changes that enhance fairness and opportunity for all employees.

For example, instead of boasting about a single high-profile diverse hire, institutions should ensure that pathways to advancement are available to all employees, regardless of background, and that these pathways are based on demonstrated skills and contributions.

5. **Holding DEI Programs Accountable**: Just as any other department within an organization is subject to accountability measures, DEI programs must also be held to account for their effectiveness. Instituting performance metrics and transparency in these programs will ensure they deliver on their stated goals and do not become a permanent drain on institutional resources.

Institutions could require DEI departments to submit annual reports detailing their goals, actions taken, and measurable outcomes. By applying the same standards of accountability as other departments, organizations can ensure that DEI efforts contribute positively to institutional health rather than becoming an unchecked bureaucracy.

THE PATH FORWARD

Navigating and countering bureaucracies that cater to DEI agendas requires a balance of pragmatism, resilience, and commitment to core principles like merit, open dialogue, and accountability. While DEI initiatives were originally intended to foster inclusivity and address inequities, their overreach has led to many unintended consequences, from stifling free speech to diminishing meritocracy.

The path forward lies in restoring balance. This means reasserting the value of individual achievement, encouraging honest and open discussions about the limitations of DEI, and ensuring that bureaucracies do not become ideological echo chambers that undermine the institutions they aim to serve. By demanding better from both individuals and institutions, we can foster environments where diversity and merit coexist, where fairness is practiced rather than preached, and where resilience and responsibility are the hallmarks of personal and collective success.

CHAPTER FOURTEEN

RESILIENCE IN A MODERN WORLD

As we come to the final chapter, it's important to reflect on the central themes that have carried us through this exploration of Gen Z—a generation both plagued by challenges and blessed with unique opportunities. We've discussed generational cycles, the shifting values of society, the role of technology, and the pressures of modern culture. But now, it's time to look forward: how can we inspire resilience and redefine a future that embraces both progress and personal accountability?

GENERATIONAL CYCLES AND HISTORICAL PARALLELS

History often repeats itself, and each generation follows a cycle of struggle, success, and eventual complacency. Sir John Glubb's model reminds us that empires and societies, much like generations, go through stages of development, peak, and decline. Gen Z is not exempt from this pattern—they face their own struggles, but they also hold the potential to redefine the values of society in a profound way. They are a part of this historical rhythm, yet their actions can choose to break from it, to chart a new course that carries humanity towards growth and renewal rather than decline.

FROM RESILIENCE TO FRAGILITY

The story of modern society is often one of fragility. We have gone from a world where resilience and sacrifice were fundamental, to a time where wealth and comfort have sometimes eroded the values that allowed society to thrive. The central thesis of this book has explored how wealth and progress, though desirable, have often led to an entitled mindset and a loss of resilience. But this shift is not irreversible. History is full of examples of societies that found their way back from decline by embracing change and committing to rebuilding. Gen Z — you have the chance to do just that.

TECHNOLOGY'S ROLE

Technology influences every modern generation. For Gen Z, technology has been a double-edged sword. On the one hand, it has brought global awareness, an unprecedented ability to mobilize for change, and a wealth of information. It has led to an overreliance on external validation, mental health challenges, and a diluted sense of real-world connection. Just as previous generations adapted to introducing new technologies, whether it was the printing press, radio, or television, too must Gen Z learn to harness technology for its positive potential, while avoiding its pitfalls.

ECONOMIC PRESSURES AND CULTURAL CONTEXT

To understand the attitudes of Gen Z, we must also acknowledge the pressures they have faced: the lingering effects of the 2008 financial crisis, the realities of rising economic inequality, and the existential anxiety surrounding climate change. These factors have created a cultural context that differs from any previous generation. However, recognizing these challenges is only the beginning. True progress comes from understanding how to navigate through them, how to rise above these circumstances with grit and determination.

ACKNOWLEDGING THE STRENGTHS OF GEN Z

While much of this book has critiqued the pitfalls of Gen Z, it's essential to recognize the positive contributions they have made to society. Gen Z is a generation of activists. They have taken up the mantle of climate change, diversity, and inclusion, not just with words but with action. Their digital fluency allows them to organize, to make their voices heard, and to influence change on a global scale. Their activism is not just a trend, it is a genuine expression of their desire to see a better future.

Gen Z is also characterized by empathy. Their focus on mental health, their advocacy for human rights, and their deep awareness of social issues are evidence of a generation that cares deeply about the world. These values, while sometimes misunderstood or criticized, come from a place of wanting to create a future that is fairer and more compassionate.

HISTORICAL LESSONS AND INSPIRATIONS

We have much to learn from previous generations. The Greatest Generation faced hardships we can barely imagine today—the Great Depression, World War II, and the need for unity in the face of adversity. What carried them through those times was a spirit of sacrifice, a willingness to work hard, and an unyielding resilience. The stories of individuals who rose above their circumstances—whether they were civil rights leaders, war heroes, or entrepreneurs—serve as powerful examples of what is possible when resilience is prioritized over comfort.

BUILDING RESILIENCE: A PRACTICAL APPROACH

Resilience is not an abstract concept; it can be cultivated, developed, and strengthened over time. For Gen Z, the journey towards resilience begins with actionable steps:

- **Embrace Discomfort**: Growth never comes from staying comfortable. Take on challenges that push you beyond what you think you can handle—whether it's through volunteer work, taking on leadership roles, or pursuing projects that seem daunting. Seek discomfort, because that is where true growth happens.

- **Develop a Growth Mindset:** See failures as opportunities to learn, not as defining moments. The willingness to get back up after falling is the essence of resilience. Adopting a growth mindset means understanding that your abilities are not fixed—you can grow, adapt, and overcome any obstacle.

- **Limit Social Media Usage**: Disconnect from the constant need for external validation that social media often fuels. Real world relationships, personal accomplishments, and offline experiences are where true self-worth is cultivated. Learn to balance your digital and offline lives and use technology as a tool rather than a crutch.

- **Mental Health Strategies**: Resilience also requires mental fortitude. Embrace mindfulness, practice self-reflection, and seek out therapy if needed. Strengthening internal resilience is about building a support system within yourself, not relying solely on external structures.

THE ROLE OF SOCIETY AND INSTITUTIONS

Resilience is not just an individual pursuit; it requires the support of society. Our educational systems must evolve to encourage critical thinking, problem-solving, and emotional intelligence. Communities must foster a sense of belonging and shared responsibility. Employers need to challenge their employees while also providing the environment for personal and professional growth. These changes are essential for cultivating a culture of resilience that goes beyond individual efforts.

ADDRESSING COUNTERARGUMENTS

Some argue that the challenges faced by Gen Z are unique and insurmountable. But while each generation faces its own set of circumstances, the core challenge of building resilience is universal. Economic insecurity, mental health struggles, and societal pressures are not new — they have been experienced by previous generations as well. Gen Z's challenges may be different in their specifics, but the path to overcoming them is the same: resilience, adaptability, and willingness to work through adversity.

WOKENESS AND CANCEL CULTURE

Social justice movements, while often criticized for their excesses, address legitimate concerns. However, there is a danger in embracing ideological rigidity that prevents constructive dialogue. Resilience also means being willing to engage with those who think differently, to listen, and to grow through conversations that challenge your worldview. Social justice does not have to come at the expense of resilience; it can be strengthened by it.

A BROADER CALL TO ACTION

To truly create a culture of resilience, we need action from all sectors of society. Leaders and policymakers must prioritize initiatives that offer young people opportunities to thrive, such as tackling student debt, making housing affordable, and creating jobs that offer both challenge and security. Communities and families must model the values of resilience and collective responsibility, mentoring young people and giving them space to develop independence.

We also need a cultural shift—one that balances social progress with personal accountability. Moving away from a culture of victimhood, we must celebrate perseverance, strength, and the ability to rise above adversity. These values must be at the core of our collective identity if we are to create a society that thrives.

THE PATH FORWARD

In closing, there is hope for the future. Gen Z faces challenges that no previous generation has had to contend with, but they also have unprecedented tools at their disposal. Technology, global connectivity, and a deep sense of social awareness are powerful assets that can be used to create positive change. But progress is not the responsibility of one generation alone. It is a collective effort—one that requires everyone, young and old, to contribute to building a resilient, inclusive, and sustainable society.

History is filled with cycles of rise and decline, but the future is not predetermined. Each generation has the power to break patterns, to redefine what is possible, and to foster a renewal of values like hard work, discipline, and responsibility. The resilience demonstrated by those who came before us can be reignited if we choose to prioritize it. The power to shape the future lies not in comfort but in courage, and it is this courage that will ultimately define what Gen Z—and all of us—can achieve.

About the Author

Patrick Bass is an author and respected radio host known for his fearless critique of modern social issues and his ability to confront difficult subjects head-on. With nearly 30 years of experience in cybersecurity, business, and education, Patrick brings a unique perspective to the conversation, blending insights from his varied career.

Patrick is also the author of two other compelling books: 'Burn Your Ships: How to Conquer Doubt and Live Without Limits' and 'The Modern Gentleman: A Guide to Essential Manhood.' In these works, he in-spires readers to overcome obstacles and embrace their fullest potential.

When he's not writing, Patrick is inspiring audiences as the host of The Patrick Bass Show, a daily talk show that uncovers the extraordinary and explores the mysteries that shape our world.

Whether through his books, his blog, or his radio shows, Patrick Bass continues to challenge the status quo, encouraging readers and listeners alike to look be-yond the surface and think critically about the world around them. He resides in Fort Smith, Arkansas, where he continues to write, explore new ideas, and in-spire others to live without limits.

For more information, to purchase books, or listen to the talk show, **visit www.pwbass.com**.